The Future of Wireless: Speeding Up Without Losing Signal

Shiva

TABLE OF CONTENTS

CHAPTER 1

INTRODUCTION

Wireless communication systems have seen tremendous innovation since their inception by Marconi, who invented the first ever functional radio transmitter (TX) and receiver (RX), around the year 1895. Since that time, wireless applications have proliferated, and the continuous need for higher throughput and lower latency has driven the development of more-capable wireless communication systems. Commercial wireless applications, nonetheless, have mostly depended on lower frequency spectrum—below 6 GHz—except maybe for satellite and radar systems. Low-frequency electromagnetic signals have had such dominance because of their favorable propagation characteristics. For instance, they are able to travel longer distances (compared to high-frequency signals) and they have higher penetration power, i.e., they can travel through walls and buildings. Moreover, in a typical setting, a low-frequency signal transmitted from one point in space can reach its destination through many distinct paths, which creates a "rich scattering" environment. This is extremely beneficial in Multiple-Input Multiple-Output (MIMO) antenna systems since the channel capacity and spatial diversity scale with the number of used antennas, for the same amount of bandwidth.

Towards high-frequency systems: The main drawback of low-frequency communication, however, is that the available bandwidth is very limited. This scarcity of spectrum resources constitutes a bottleneck on the growth of wireless communication networks. An obvious solution to the spectrum shortage problem is the utilization of higher frequencies, specifically, the millimeter-wave (mmWave) spectrum band, where orders of magnitude more spectrum resources are available [1–4]. MmWave refers to the spectrum band in which the wavelength is measured in units of millimeters. More precisely, at frequencies between 30 and 300 GHz. Inevitably, next-generation wireless networks, armed with more capable transceiver designs, are increasingly headed towards exploiting mmWave frequencies. This development trend, despite being bound by the same challenges that have limited the utilization of high frequencies for decades, holds a great potential due to: (1) the availability of vastly under-utilized spectrum resources, and (2) the increased accessibility of the sophisticated technologies required to make such systems commercially viable. Nonetheless, due to the significant challenges facing mmWave, its early system deployments have either relied on lower frequency spectrum for control signaling or have been restricted to low mobility settings, e.g., Fixed-Access Networks. Next, we will discuss the role mmWave systems play in future networks and discuss the challenges that need to be overcome for such systems to be more versatile.

MmWave in next-generation networks: Perhaps the most obvious example of the advancement of wireless systems is the evolution of cellular networks. In 2019, the 5th generation networks, i.e., 5G New Radio (5G-NR), started being rolled out. 5G promises peak throughput in units of Gbps, and latency below 1 ms. These specifications will not only enable an enhanced Mobile Broad Band (MBB) user experience, but will also extend 5G applications to massive Machine-Type Communications (m-MTC) and Ultra Reliable Low Latency Communications (URLLC). The key to attaining such hopeful performance requirements is to utilize the largely untapped spectrum resources in the mmWave spectrum band, also known in 5G jargon as Frequency Range 2 (FR2). FR1, on the other hand, refers to the spectrum below 6

GHz (now extended to 7 GHz). At the present time, 5G networks still depend on FR1 for Control Plane signaling due to its higher reliability compared to FR2. A revolutionary mmWave-exclusive cellular system has not been realized as of yet due to the challenges surrounding the use of high frequency signals.

Another class of networks which started employing mmWave technology is Wireless Local Area Networks (WLAN), with its most common brand WiFi. The newer WiFi standards of IEEE 802.11ad/ay (i.e., WiGig) will operate on the unlicensed 60 GHz frequency band. This will enable a massive increase in data throughput, and could even pave the way for these new WiFi standards to replace Ethernet cables as the new go-to wireless solution. Its applications can also reach Extended Reality (XR), which is expected to require hundreds of Gbps speeds and low latency. Nonetheless, these new WiFi standards still do not handle user mobility well due to the constant changing nature of the channels and the relatively large overhead required for channel estimation and channel tracking. Hence, faster link establishment between users and Access Points, compared to the state-of-the-art solutions, as well as faster channel tracking need to be developed.

Challenges facing mmWave systems: The propagation characteristics of high-frequency electromagnetic signals are, nonetheless, poor [5]. For instance, according to Friis transmission equation, the received power, in free space, is inversely proportional to the frequency squared. Furthermore, atmospheric absorption over certain frequency bands (e.g. 24 and 60 GHz) can significantly increase transmission losses. Hence, signals only travel limited distances. Moreover, high-frequency signals do not penetrate obstacles like building and trees very well. These qualities make it very challenging for wireless systems to utilize high-frequency signals. But there is light at the end of the tunnel as new technologies make it possible to overcome those shortcomings.

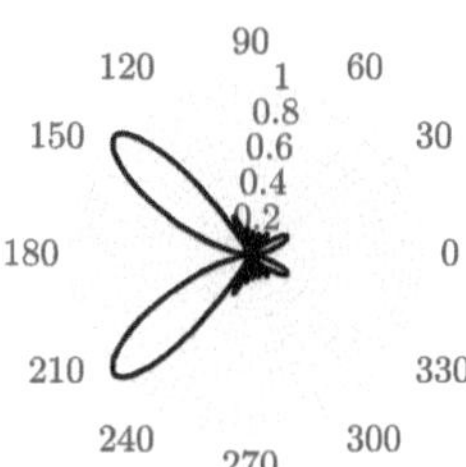

Figure 1.1: High-gain antenna beam pattern example (using 15 antennas)

Benefits of mmWave systems: While the aforementioned factors impose serious challenges to adopting mmWave, they also provides advantages in terms of better spectrum reuse and spacial multiplexing, hence improving the overall spectrum utilization of the system. Moreover, there obviously exists a vast amount of available spectrum, which solves the main problem of low-frequency systems. More interestingly, the key to overcome the severe path loss problem of mmWave is also due to its high-frequency. Since at high frequency we have short wavelength. And since the spacing of antenna elements in mobile devices is limited by the wavelength of the carrier frequency (i.e., antennas are placed half a wavelength apart (critical spacing)). Then, we are able to pack more antenna elements in hand-held mobile devices. That is, we are able to utilize large phased-antenna arrays, which, in turn, provides large antenna gains (beamforming gains) at the transmitter (TX) and receiver (RX). Severe path losses can thus be compensated for using these large antenna arrays [1]. Fig. 1.1 shows an example of a high-gain directional antenna beam with 15 elements.

Large antenna arrays, transceiver architecture and channel estimation: Traditional transceiver architectures have mostly adopted a fully-digital design. In digital architectures, each antenna element is connected to a dedicated RF chain with its own mixers, filters, ADCs/DACs, etc. High frequency electronic components, however, are costly and consumes a lot of power [6]. Hence, a fully-digital transceiver with a large antenna array would be both extremely power-hungry and very expensive to build. Therefore, mmWave systems have to abandon the classical fully-digital transceiver architecture in favor of cheaper power-efficient designs. Besides, digital transceivers are not actually needed in order to achieve the channel capacity, owing to the fact that mmWave channels are sparse (i.e., they only contain few channel paths compared to the channel dimensions) [3, 7, 8]. Alternative practical transceivers architectures are henceforth adopted including: simple analog transceivers (with one RF chain connected to all antenna elements using phase-shifters), and hybrid transceivers (with multiple RF chains, each connected to all antenna elements using phase-shifters) [9–11], among other architectures. Ideas of using a digital transceiver but with low resolution ADCs (possibly one bit resolution) have also been explored [12–14].

To efficiently utilize the large antenna arrays, channel state information (CSI) needs to be available at both transceiver ends. This creates another serious challenge. Specifically, large antenna arrays produces large channel matrices, which would need to be estimated before data transmission can take place. The large size of the channel matrices, in particular, makes this problem complex. This problem is further exacerbated by the limited capabilities of the considered transceivers.

An alternative way of looking at the channel estimation problem is that the TX and RX would need to align their antenna beams such that the benefits of high antenna gains could be reaped. Due to the large number of possible alignment combinations, this process could waste valuable transmission opportunities and form a bottleneck on the performance of mmWave systems. In mobile environments where the channel is constantly changing, channel estimation is carried out more frequently, which aggravates the large overhead problem.

Channel sparsity and the path to fewer measurements: Measurement campaigns have revealed that mmWave channels exhibit a spare structure, where the transmitted signal by TX reaches the destination (RX) along a few number of paths [3, 7, 15]. Channel paths are found in clusters[1] in the angular domain, where a very limited number of clusters exist. Hence, we can represent the channel in a domain (i.e., the angular domain) where most of the channel components vanish (i.e., are negligibly small). The prior information we have about typical mmWave channel structures allows us to discover the channel matrix using fewer measurements than would otherwise be necessary, which is crucial for reducing the estimation overhead. The sparsity of mmWave channels also means that channel capacity is limited by the rank of the channel matrix rather than the number of TX and RX antennas. This provides another rationale for ditching the digital transceiver architecture.

Most existing channel estimation solutions rely on compressed Sensing to reduce the number of channel measurements [9, 16–18]. These solutions largely depend on random beamforming in order to collect random independent measurements of the channel. Other approaches include: i) measurements with hierarchical beam patterns that sequentially narrow down the angular direction(s) which contain strong propagation paths, ii) measurements with randomly overlapped beam patterns where each measurement combines signals received from a randomly selected set of angular directions [19], and iii) machine learning based algorithms for sparse recovery of mmWave channels [20–23]. Related work is more thoroughly discussed in Section 1.2.

---

[1]A *cluster* refers to a propagation path or continuum of paths that span a small interval of transmit Angles of Departure (AoD) and receive Angles of Arrival (AoA).

In this book, we propose a different, deterministic approach to sparse chan-nel estimation, that is based on "binary coding". Our solution is motivated by the shortcomings of randomized measurements adopted by state-of-the-art solutions and is inspired by analogies we draw from the binary *channel coding* and binary *source coding* problems. We also propose a new measurement-to-channel mapping frame-work which breaks down the complex problem of estimating the channel matrix into smaller simpler sub-problems that can be run in parallel, hence enhancing the speed of measurement processing. Finally, we study the basic limits governing the number of measurements, which is crucial for understanding the nature of this problem.

Problem Description: The mmWave channel estimation problem can generally be divided into two intertwined parts. The first is: ***how to obtain "good" mea-surements that can be used to reliably discover the channel?*** and the second is: ***how to map these measurements to corresponding channel estimates?*** Motivated by our proposed solutions, as will shortly be introduced, we name these two parts *"Channel Encoding"* and *"Measurement Decoding"*, respectively. Encoding and decoding are intertwined because a selection of a specific decoding method often dictates (i) how the measurements are obtained, and (ii) the number of measurements for which this specific decoding method would yield "good" performance. The disso-ciation of encoding and decoding as two sub-problems can be seen across almost all mmWave channel estimation research, albeit not always explicitly mentioned. This distinction, however, facilitates the identification of key aspects upon which we could improve the quality of channel estimation.

A well-known classification of encoding paradigms is encoding *with* vs. *without* feedback. Non-feedback encoding is better suited for simultaneous multi-user channel estimation, hence is scalable, while feedback-based encoding operates better at low

SNR [24]. Different decoding algorithms are also needed for these two types. This book focuses on encoding without feedback.

1.1 Contributions

In this book, we thoroughly tackle the problem of estimating sparse large-MIMO channels (a class which includes mmWave channels). While doing so, we consider practical *energy-efficient* transceiver architectures and propose estimation techniques, rooted in *binary coding*, that accurately recover the channel matrix, yet only require *few deterministic measurements*. The deterministic nature of our mea-surement framework yields a precise value for the number of required channel mea-surements, results in uniformly-shaped antenna beamforming patterns, and exhibits superior channel estimation performance compared to state-of-the-art solutions.

In Chapter 3, we derive an analogy between sparse channel estimation and the linear block coding problem. Linear block codes are used to discover and correct for errors that sparsely occur in blocks of fixed-size binary sequences upon transmission (or storage) over a noisy channel. Similarly, we show that the same codes can be used to discover channel paths that are sparsely represented in the channel. We will start by describing the problem in a simple Single-Input Multiple-Output antenna setting. Then, we show that we can obtain unique channel measurements for every possible channel. Afterwards, we consider the general MIMO channel setting.

Since the channel matrix is large in size, its recovery from the smaller number of acquired measurements remains a complex task. This problem alone has been the focus of many research works, usually tackled under the umbrella of compressed sensing. In this chapter, however, we lay down the foundation of a novel framework that breaks down the complex problem of recovering the channel matrix from the obtained measurements into several smaller sub-problems, each is designed to recover a specific row or a column of the channel matrix. These sub-problems are run in two subsequent stages, but in each stage, all sub-problems can be run in parallel, which can dramatically increase the speed of processing.

In Chapter 4, we focus our efforts on understanding the fundamental limits governing the mmWave channel estimation problem under our binary-coding-based solution. Specifically, we seek to find a *lower bound* on the number of measurements, which can be used to find "good" channel estimates. We accomplish this task by drawing another, more direct analogy between sparse MIMO channel estimation and the problem of binary source compression/coding. The number of measurements under this framework is proportional to the compression ratio of the used binary code. Hence, a lower bound on the compression ratio, which can be easily derived using the Shannon bound, provides a straight-forward bound on the number of measurements.

We also propose a machine-learning-based measurement decoding solution which dramatically enhances the speed of channel estimation while producing near-optimal results. This solution can be plugged in the framework introduced in Chapter 3 to solve each of the measurement-to-channel mapping sub-problems, providing an order of magnitude increase in speed.

Finally, in Chapter 5 we assess the efficiency of measurement reduction of our framework by comparing the asymptotic scaling of our obtained bound in Chapter 3 to the corresponding **general** asymptotic lower bound for this problem. We observe that the best known general bound is a lot smaller than our framework's bound, but a closer inspection reveals that the general bound in question does not account for the intricate details of the MIMO channel estimation problem. This motivates us to derive a tighter general bound that is tailored for MIMO channel estimation. Interestingly, our new tight bound scales exactly as the lower bound for our proposed solution. More crucially, however, it also serves as a benchmark for evaluating any proposed solution for sparse large-MIMO channel estimation.

We summarize our contributions in this **book** as follows:

- We propose a deterministic framework for sparse large-MIMO channel estimation that is based on *linear* binary coding problems.

- Our solution works on a simple power-efficient analog transceiver.

- We characterize two tight lower bounds on the number of measurements: the first is specific for our proposed solution, while the second is general and can be applied for any solution. Both bounds have the same asymptotic scaling.

- We present a new measurement-to-channel mapping framework which breaks down the channel matrix estimation to smaller parallelizable sub-problems. Different solutions can be used to solve these sub-problems including a proposed Deep Learning based method, which greatly enhances the speed of computation.

1.2 Related Work

The main objective of mmWave channel estimation is to find a mechanism that can reliably estimate the channel using as few measurements as possible. Based on prior information about the channel, two classes of channel estimation paradigms exist, namely, Initial Access and Channel/Beam Tracking.

Initial Access: The "Initial Access" problem is concerned with finding the angular bearings of one or more propagation paths between a pair of TX and RX nodes, without prior knowledge about previous channel values. In mobile environments, these angular directions are expected to change after Initial Access. "Beam Tracking" methods are commonly used to correct for smaller angular changes and maintain the viability of active link(s) [25, 26]. Nonetheless, due to the narrow beams at both TX and RX, established communication links are prone to blockage (by objects in the communication environment, and even the users themselves). Hence, the initial link establishment stage might need to be repeated multiple times during every communication session. This results in high overhead for establishing coherent beams during the course of the session, if the initial access process is inefficient. This book focuses on the Initial Access problem.

Compressed Sensing (CS): In CS theory, the main objective is to recover an unknown *sparse vector* q^a using a small number (compared to the sparse vector dimensions) of linear measurements. Measurements in CS, denoted by y, are modeled as $y = Bq^a$, where B is the sensing matrix. Hence, B is a linear transformation that amounts to encoding q^a. Sparse recovery algorithms, on the other hand, amount to decoding y. To obtain "good" measurements (which best preserve the information contained in the channel matrix), the sensing matrix need to be stochastically optimized based on criteria like the spark(B) (i.e., minimum number of linearly dependent columns), the mutual coherence and the Restricted Isometry Property.

Since mmWave channel matrices are sparse, and since channel measurements are linear operations, CS became a dominant approach for tackling mmWave channel estimation problems. The main caveat here is that the standard CS problem is that of a sparse vector recovery, while mmWave channel estimation is a sparse matrix recovery. This distinction poses some challenges in tackling mmWave channel estimation under the umbrella of CS. To formulate MIMO channel estimation as a CS problem, a vectorization step is carried out (i.e., columns of matrices are stacked on top of each other to form one long vector). Nonetheless, unlike standard CS problems in which elements of the sensing matrices are directly chosen and optimized, the mmWave sensing matrix is a function of the transmit precoding and receive combining vectors.

This adds an extra layer of complexity which is often ignored under the premise that since CS often requires random sensing matrices, then random beamforming is an obvious necessity. However, it is not immediately clear how a specific choice of precoders and combiners would affect the structure of $\boldsymbol{B}$, and therefore, the performance of sparse recovery. Extending the design principles of sensing matrices from core CS theory to mmWave channel estimation is thus not straightforward and remains an open area of research.

Existing research on CS-based mmWave channel estimation relies on ***random*** arbitrary choices of precoding and combining vectors, e.g. uniformly distributed phase shifts [27, 28]. When this solution is incorporated in mmWave channel estimation, it translates into designing antenna beam patterns of highly irregular shapes (see Fig. 4.5). Such beam patterns are sensitive to variations of received signal power, thermal noise and resolution of ADCs and phase-shifters. Our proposed source-coding-based solution overcomes these limitations by imposing better, well-structured antenna patterns, where, in each measurement, a specific angular direction is either included (with constant beamforming gain) or is excluded. This provides better resilience to i) the presence of sidelobes, ii) variations in received signal power along any available path(s), iii) channel noise and iv) quantization error of ADCs and phase shifters. Furthermore, the deterministic nature of our measurements allows us to provide theoretical guarantees for channel recovery at a precise number of measurements. This will be achieved by creating analogies to the problems of (1) binary channel coding, and (2) binary source coding. The source coding analogy also allows us to draw theoretical tight lower bounds on the number of measurements.

On the contrary, the number of required measurements in CS is commonly characterized as an order of magnitude. For instance, several state-of-the-art sparse recovery algorithms require $O(L \log(\frac{n}{L}))$ measurements, where n is the number of dimensions of the sparse vector and $L \ll n$ is its sparsity level [9, 16]. This, however, is just a scaling law, which by definition, works in the asymptotic regime and is missing the constant scaling coefficient. Compare this to our solution, which accurately specifies the required number of measurements (based on n and L).

Developing efficient sparse recovery algorithms for CS-based mmWave channel estimation is a rich area of research. Various algorithms have different computational complexities, recovery performance, favorable range of signal to noise ratio (SNR), etc. A comparison between several classes of sparse recovery algorithms is provided in [28]. These include convex relaxation (e.g. l_1-norm minimization), greedy iteration (e.g. Orthogonal Matching Pursuit (OMP)) and Bayesian Inference. Other algorithms also include Approximate Message Passing (AMP) [29] and its variants [30], as well as machine learning based sparse recovery [31].

Machine Learning: Deep learning is very powerful in extracting patterns from large amounts of data. It has been widely used in problems of computer vision, speech recognition and natural language processing. Recently, it has also been applied to problems in communications [32], including, but not limited to channel estimation [21–23]. For instance, in [23] the beamforming vectors at the TX and RX are *"learned"* based on uplink pilot signals simultaneously received at multiple base stations. The base stations share their received information on a cloud, on which data processing is performed. This idea is critically dependent on a dense deployment of base stations. In [21, 22], deep learning is leveraged to ease the burden of heavy computations that would otherwise be required for measurement processing. In Chapter 4, we will use a classical Deep Neural Network to perform a similar goal where DNNs are used to map the collection of obtained measurements to a corresponding channel estimate.

Hashed Beams: An idea of generating antenna beam patterns which follows the method of direction inclusion/exclusion is adopted in [19]. Specifically, every measurement combines signals coming from a ***randomly*** chosen set of angular directions. Our proposed solutions in Chapters 3 and 4 follow a similar direction inclusion/exclusion pattern, except that the angular directions included in any particular measurement are based on a deterministic, appropriately chosen binary code. The measurement design in [19] is a random channel encoding method and it resembles a *random* binary code. For measurement-to-channel mapping, i.e., measurement decoding, a threshold-based decision determines whether a strong propagation path exists (if a path exists, it lies at one of the directions included in this measurement). The direction which was most frequently included in the measurements that revealed a strong path is declared as the angular direction of the strongest channel path. This method discovers one path, and requires $O(L\log(n))$ measurements. In our proposed approach, the angular directions whose respective beams are overlapped are ***precisely determined*** using a carefully chosen code. We also use an elaborate decoding method that is capable of discovering multiple channel paths. Our solution guarantees a lower number of measurements since a randomly chosen code is not expected to outperform a carefully designed one.

Using phase information: Most research efforts in the field of mmWave channel estimation use the magnitude and phase information of the acquired channel measurements. Nevertheless, if a carrier frequency offset (CFO) error occurs in the transceiver hardware, the phase information might be unreliable. Hence, the work in [33–35] tackle this problem by ignoring the phase information. Similar to [33, 34], the solution in [35] can only obtain one (dominant) path between TX and RX using a compressed sensing based technique. The CFO problem is tackled in [36] by considering it as a variable to be estimated.

Transceiver architectures: While the power consumption problem of mmWave systems is commonly alleviated using analog and hybrid transceivers, an alternative solution is to use low-resolution ADCs in fully-digital architectures. Owing to the fact that low-resolution ADCs operate at much lower power than their high-resolution counterparts, the work in [12–14, 37] employ low-resolution (single-bit) ADCs in digital transceivers. The work in [38, 39] study the channel estimation problem using such architectures. Other solutions include integrated mmWave and sub-6 GHz systems [40] to provide reliable and energy efficient communication systems.

1.3 Notations

Let x be a scalar quantity—real or complex depending on the context—and let $\boldsymbol{x}$ be a vector while $\boldsymbol{X}$ be a matrix. The conjugate of $\boldsymbol{X}$ is $\boldsymbol{X}^*$, its transpose is $\boldsymbol{X}^T$, its hermition (i.e., conjugate transpose) is $\boldsymbol{X}^H$ and its Frobenius norm is $\|\boldsymbol{X}\|_F$. Let $\|\boldsymbol{x}\|_p$ denote the pth norm of $\boldsymbol{x}$. If the subscript p is dropped, then $\|\boldsymbol{x}\|$ denotes the Euclidean norm, $\|\boldsymbol{x}\|_2$. Define the operator $\text{vec}(\boldsymbol{X})$ to be the stacking of all the columns of $\boldsymbol{X}$ to form one vector as follows: If $\boldsymbol{X}$ has columns $\boldsymbol{x}_i$ for $i = 1, \ldots, n$, then $\text{vec}(\boldsymbol{X}) = \left(\boldsymbol{x}_1^T \ \ \boldsymbol{x}_2^T \ \ \ldots \ \ \boldsymbol{x}_n^T \right)^T$.

The sets of real and complex numbers are denoted by $\mathbb{R}$ and $\mathbb{C}$. The $k \times k$ identity matrix is $\boldsymbol{I}_k$. A set is denoted by $\mathcal{X}$, while $|\mathcal{X}|$ is its cardinality. Define $\mathbb{1}_{\{\cdot\}}$ to be the indicator function which takes a value of 1 when the condition in the subscript is satisfied, and 0 otherwise. We denote by $\otimes$ the Kronecker product. Finally, we use: (i) $\Omega(\cdot)$ to denote the Big Omega notation, i.e., the asymptotic lower bound[2], (ii) $O(\cdot)$ to denote the Big O notation, i.e., the asymptotic upper bound[3], and (iii) we say that $f(n) \in \Theta(g(n))$ if both $f(n) \in \Omega(g(n))$ and $f(n) \in O(g(n))$.

---

[2] We say that $f(n) \in \Omega(g(n))$ (or loosely, $f(n){=}\Omega(g(n))$) if there exists a constant $c > 0$, and $n_0 \in \mathbb{N}$ such that $f(n) \geq cg(n)$, for all $n{\geq}n_0$.

[3] We say that $f(n) \in O(g(n))$ (or loosely $f(n){=}O(g(n))$) if there exists a constant $c > 0$ and $n_0 \in \mathbb{N}$ such that $f(n) \leq cg(n)$, for all $n{\geq}n_0$.

CHAPTER 2

SYSTEM MODEL

We consider point-to-point mmWave channels with n_t and n_r antennas at TX and RX, respectively. Antennas at TX/RX form Uniform Linear Arrays (ULA). Generalization to Uniform Planar Arrays is straightforward but not considered in this work for simplicity. Every antenna element is connected to a phase-shifter and a low-power variable-gain amplifier (VGA)[1]. On the TX side, a single RF chain feeds its ULA through an n_t-way power splitter, while on the RX side, the outputs of the ULA, after being processed by amplifiers and phase-shifters, are linearly combined using an adder and fed through to a single RF chain with in-phase (I) and quadrature (Q) channels. Two mid-tread ADCs with 2^b+1 levels are used to quantize the I and Q components of the received signal. The term b loosely denotes the number of bits that describe the ADC resolution. Fig. 2.1 depicts the transceiver architecture.

We assume single-tap channels. We also adopt a channel clustering model where paths between TX and RX form clusters in the angular domain [1, 7]. Due to the sparse nature of mmWave channels [31, 43–47], only a limited number of clusters exist[2]. Let L denote the number of available channel clusters, and let k denote the

---

[1]The use of VGAs in analog transceivers is common in practice. For instance, in IEEE 802.11ad [41] both phase and amplitude components are used to specify antenna weights, and commercial devices like Wilocity Wil6200 offer this capability. VGAs are also used along with phase-shifters in practice to help compensate for their phase-dependent insertion loss [42].

[2]Prior knowledge about the number of clusters can be obtained from statistical channel information,

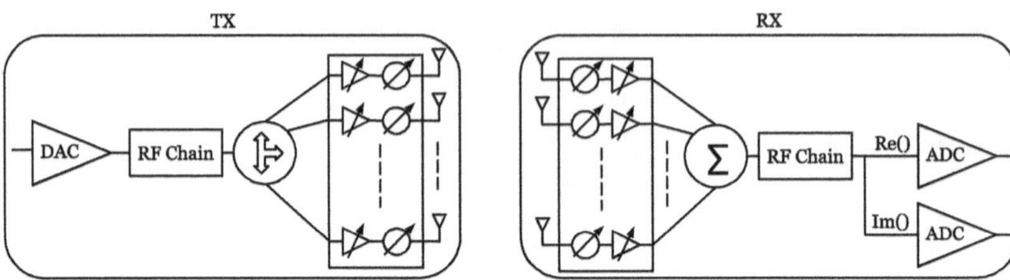

Figure 2.1: Transceiver architecture: At TX, an n_t-way power splitter divides the transmit signal which is then passed through variable-gain amplifiers and phase-shifters. A single DAC is required since TX sends real valued signals. At RX, the acquired signal is passed through a similar network of power amplifiers and phase-shifters before being combined and fed to a single RF chain. Two ADCs are required to obtain I/Q components of received signals.

maximum number of *resolvable* signal propagation paths in the channel. By the sparsity assumption, we have that $L, k \ll n_r, n_t$. Note that a wireless transceiver may not be able to resolve multiple channel paths if they are spatially close and the antenna beam-widths are not small enough to resolve each path separately. In such case, we assume that $L = k$, i.e., every cluster is assumed to contain only one channel path. However, as the number of antennas increases, the transceiver's ability to resolve more paths also increases due to its ability to form narrower antenna beams. This means that k increases with n. However, the ratio $\dfrac{k}{n}$ decreases as n increases. We assume that $n_t, n_r \geq k^{1+\epsilon}$, for some $\epsilon>0$, which reflects the ability of transceivers to resolve more channel paths as their number of antennas increases.

Each channel path (e.g., p^{th} path) is attributed with an AoD θ_p, an AoA ϕ_p and

---

which in turn are obtained from channel measurement campaigns. For instance, measurements carried out in New York City revealed that an average number of 2 or 3 clusters exists in mmWave channels at 28 and 73 GHz [3].

a path gain α_p. Let $\alpha_p^b \in \mathbb{C}$ denote the baseband path gain such that

$$\alpha_p^b = \alpha_p \sqrt{n_r n_t} e^{-j \frac{2\pi \rho_p}{\lambda_c}}, \tag{2.0.1}$$

where ρ_p is the path length and λ_c is the carrier wavelength. We define the *directional cosines* of the AoD and AoA of the pth path as $\Omega_{tp} \triangleq \cos(\theta_p)$ and $\Omega_{rp} \triangleq \cos(\phi_p)$, respectively. The transmit and receive spatial signatures at an arbitrary directional cosine Ω is denoted by $\boldsymbol{e_t}(\Omega)$ and $\boldsymbol{e_r}(\Omega)$, receptively. We define $\boldsymbol{e_t}(\Omega)$ and $\boldsymbol{e_r}(\Omega)$ as:

$$\boldsymbol{e_t}(\Omega) = \frac{1}{\sqrt{n_t}} \begin{pmatrix} 1 \\ e^{-j2\pi\Delta_t\Omega} \\ e^{-j2\pi 2\Delta_t\Omega} \\ \vdots \\ e^{-j2\pi(n_t-1)\Delta_t\Omega} \end{pmatrix}, \qquad \boldsymbol{e_r}(\Omega) = \frac{1}{\sqrt{n_r}} \begin{pmatrix} 1 \\ e^{-j2\pi\Delta_r\Omega} \\ e^{-j2\pi 2\Delta_r\Omega} \\ \vdots \\ e^{-j2\pi(n_r-1)\Delta_r\Omega} \end{pmatrix} \tag{2.0.2}$$

where Δ_t and Δ_r are antenna separations at TX and RX, normalized by λ_c.

Let $\boldsymbol{Q} \in \mathbb{C}^{n_r \times n_t}$ denote the channel matrix such that $\boldsymbol{Q} = \sum_{p=1}^{k} \alpha_p^b \boldsymbol{e_r}(\Omega_{rp}) \boldsymbol{e_t}^H(\Omega_{tp})$. The corresponding angular channel of $\boldsymbol{Q}$, whose rows and columns divide the channel into resolvable RX and TX angular bins, respectively, is denoted by $\boldsymbol{Q^a}$ and can be obtained using a simple linear transformation [48] as

$$\boldsymbol{Q^a} = \boldsymbol{U_r^H} \boldsymbol{Q} \boldsymbol{U_t}. \tag{2.0.3}$$

If n_t or n_r equals 1, $\boldsymbol{Q}$ and $\boldsymbol{Q^a}$ are reduced to vectors which we denote by $\boldsymbol{q}$ and $\boldsymbol{q^a}$, respectively. The matrices $\boldsymbol{U_t}$ and $\boldsymbol{U_r}$ are the transmit and receive *unitary Discrete Fourier Transform (DFT)* matrices whose columns form an orthonormal basis for the transmit and receive signal spaces $\mathbb{C}^{n_t}$ and $\mathbb{C}^{n_r}$, respectively. The definitions of

U_t and U_r are given by [48, Chapter 7.3.4]

$$U_t \triangleq \left(e_t\left(0\right) \quad e_t\left(\tfrac{1}{L_t}\right) \quad \cdots \quad e_t\left(\tfrac{n_t-1}{L_t}\right) \right),\tag{2.0.4}$$

$$U_r \triangleq \left(e_r\left(0\right) \quad e_r\left(\tfrac{1}{L_r}\right) \quad \cdots \quad e_r\left(\tfrac{n_r-1}{L_r}\right) \right),\tag{2.0.5}$$

where $L_t = n_t \Delta_t$ and $L_r = n_r \Delta_r$ denote the length of the TX and RX antenna arrays, respectively, normalized by λ_c.

Similar to [9, 38, 49], we assume perfect sparsity where channel paths lie along AoD and AoA directions defined in U_t and U_r. Hence, each path only contributes to a single component of Q^a. Thus, only k non-zero components exist[3] in Q^a. The baseband channel model is

$$y_b = Qx + n \tag{2.0.6}$$

where y_b is the received vector at RX front-end while $n \sim \mathcal{CN}\left(0, N_0 I_{n_r}\right)$ is an i.i.d. complex Gaussian noise vector. TX sends pilot symbols s, with power P, which are processed using precoders $f_j \in \mathbb{C}^{n_t}$ to obtain the transmit vectors $x = f_j s$. Hence, the transmit SNR is

$$\text{SNR} \triangleq \frac{P}{N_0} \times \mu, \tag{2.0.7}$$

where μ is the average path loss (which depends on the carrier frequency, atmospheric conditions, average distance between TX and RX). Note that SNR and μ are not path

---

[3]Possibly fewer than k non-zero components exist since, according to our definition, k is the maximum number of paths we expect to find in the channel and not the actual number. The actual number of channel paths would not be known until accurate channel estimation is performed. The maximum number of channel paths can be obtained from statistical information based on measurement campaigns.

dependent. The rx-combining vectors $\boldsymbol{w}_i \in \mathbb{C}^{n_r}$ are used to obtain the received symbols $y_{i,j}$ such that

$$y_{i,j} = \boldsymbol{w}_i^H \boldsymbol{Q} \boldsymbol{f}_j s + \boldsymbol{w}_i^H \boldsymbol{n}, \qquad \text{where } i \in \{1, \ldots, m_r\}, j \in \{1, \ldots, m_t\} \tag{2.0.8}$$

Then, the total number of measurements we can obtain using all combinations of $\boldsymbol{f}_j$ and $\boldsymbol{w}_i$ is $m = m_t \times m_r$. We write the measurement equations for all precoders and combiners, more compactly, as:

$$\boldsymbol{Y} = \boldsymbol{W}^H \boldsymbol{Q} \boldsymbol{F} + \boldsymbol{N}, \tag{2.0.9}$$

where $y_{i,j}$ is the element at row i and column j of $\boldsymbol{Y}$, while $\boldsymbol{W}$ and $\boldsymbol{F}$ are defined as:

$$\boldsymbol{W} \triangleq \begin{pmatrix} \boldsymbol{w}_1 & \boldsymbol{w}_2 & \ldots & \boldsymbol{w}_{m_r} \end{pmatrix}, \tag{2.0.10}$$

$$\boldsymbol{F} \triangleq \begin{pmatrix} \boldsymbol{f}_1 & \boldsymbol{f}_2 & \ldots & \boldsymbol{f}_{m_t} \end{pmatrix} \tag{2.0.11}$$

Finally, a quantized version $u_{i,j}^s$ of $y_{i,j}$ is obtained such that

$$u_{i,j}^s = \left[\boldsymbol{w}_i^H \boldsymbol{Q} \boldsymbol{f}_j s + \boldsymbol{w}_i^H \boldsymbol{n} \right]_+ \tag{2.0.12}$$

where $[\cdot]_+$ represents the quntization function. The noise component, normalized by $\|\boldsymbol{w}_i\|$ has a complex Gaussian distribution, i.e., $\dfrac{\boldsymbol{w}_i^H \boldsymbol{n}}{\|\boldsymbol{w}_i\|} \sim \mathcal{CN}(0, N_0)$. Let $y_{i,j}^s = \boldsymbol{w}_i^H \boldsymbol{Q} \boldsymbol{f}_j s$ denote the error-free measured symbols and let $z_{i,j} = u_{i,j}^s - y_{i,j}^s$ denote the *measurement error* which includes both **channel noise** and **quantization error**.

Special Cases: Suppose the number of TX antennas $n_t = 1$. In such case, the channel is Single-Input-Multiple-Output (SIMO), and the channel matrix $\boldsymbol{Q}$ becomes a vector $\boldsymbol{q}$. The precoders at TX also fall back to just a scalar quantity; $f = 1$. Thus, we can rewrite the measurement equation (Eq. (2.0.9)) as:

$$y = W^H q + n \qquad (2.0.13)$$

Similarly, for MISO channels, i.e., $n_r{=}1$, the measurement equation becomes:

$$y = F^H q + n \qquad (2.0.14)$$

CHAPTER 3

CHANNEL MEASUREMENT BY CHANNEL CODING

3.1 Introduction

At a first glance, binary channel coding may seem a totally unrelated problem. However, we show that channel path discovery is very similar to discovering sequences of erroneous bits in Linear Block Codes (LBC). Path discovery is crucial for Initial Link Establishment between Base Stations and the users they serve. In the initial link establishment phase, we do not assume any prior knowledge about the channel except the availability of some statistical information regarding the number of channel paths.

Recall that due to the large number of antennas at TX and RX, estimation of the full channel matrix may require a large number of measurements, proportional to the product of the number of transmit and receive antennas. Reducing the number of measurements has been addressed using various methods, the most prevalent among them, is compressed sensing (CS) [9, 14, 38, 50, 51], which leverages channel sparsity. Nonetheless, the performance of compressed-sensing-based approaches is heavily dependent on the design of system (sensing) matrices, whose optimization, to the best of our knowledge, remains an open problem. In addition, despite the progress made in solving the mmWave channel estimation problem, we still do not have a full understanding of the dependence of estimation performance on the channel parameters and number of measurements. In this work, we follow a different approach, which not only advances the state-of-the-art solutions, but also sheds light on the relationship between the channel parameters and the required number of measurements.

We propose a systematic method for measurement design in which we use sequences of error correction codes chosen in a way to control the channel estimation performance. To demonstrate our approach, consider the following simple example. Let a point to point communication channel be such that, there exists 3 possible receive AoA directions, only one of which may have a strong path to TX. We need to obtain the correct AoA at RX, if it exists. Instead of exhaustively searching all 3 possible AoA directions, we alternatively measure signals from combined directions. For instance, by combining directions 1&2 in one measurement and 2&3 in the next measurement, we can find the AoA in just two measurements. Specifically, four different scenarios might occur, namely, i) only the 1st, or ii) only the 2nd measurement contains a strong path, iii) both 1st and 2nd measurements contain a strong path, and finally, iv) neither measurement reveals a strong path. Interpretation of those cases is that the AoA is in: i) direction 1, ii) direction 3, iii) direction 2, and iv) none exists. Therefore, only 2 measurements are sufficient for beam detection instead of 3 that are needed for exhaustive search.

We will generalize this idea to develop a systematic method for beam detection, inspired by linear block coding. Specifically, we show that linear block error correcting codes (LBC) possess favorable properties that fit in with the desirable behavior of sparse channel estimation. As a result, we are able to **i) provide rigorous criteria for solving the channel estimation problem, ii) significantly decrease the number of required measurements, and iii) utilize a fairly simple and energy-efficient transceiver architecture.** LBCs leverage the fact that transmission errors are typically sparse in transmitted data streams, and hence, only a few number of erroneous bits need to be corrected per transmitted codeword. Similarly, mm-wave channels are also sparse, i.e., only a small number of AoAs/AoDs carry strong signals. LBCs can correct sparse transmission errors by identifying their location in a transmitted sequence (followed by flipping them). We are inspired by LBC's ability to locate erroneous bits and exploit it to identify the AoAs/AoDs that carry strong signals (and their path gains) among all possible AoA/AoD values. To this end, we exploit hard decision decoding of LBCs, in which the receiver obtains an *error syndrome* that maps to one of the correctable error patterns. An obtained error pattern determines the positions where errors have occurred. Likewise, for channel estimation, the receiver will be designed to do a sequence of measurements that would result in a *channel syndrome*. The resultant channel syndrome shall identify the positions (and values) of non-zero angular channel components.

Our work on measurement design using binary channel codes is presented in Chapter 3. The contributions we make in this chapter can be summarized as follows:

- We set an analogy between beam discovery and channel coding to utilize low-complexity decoding techniques for efficient beam discovery.

- We provide rigorous criteria for setting the number of channel measurements based on the size of the channel and its sparsity level.

- We show that the number of measurements required for beam discovery is linked to the rate of a used linear block code. Hence, maximizing the rate of the underlying code is equivalent to minimizing the number of measurements.

- We develop a simple receiver architecture that enables us to measure signals arriving from multiple directions.

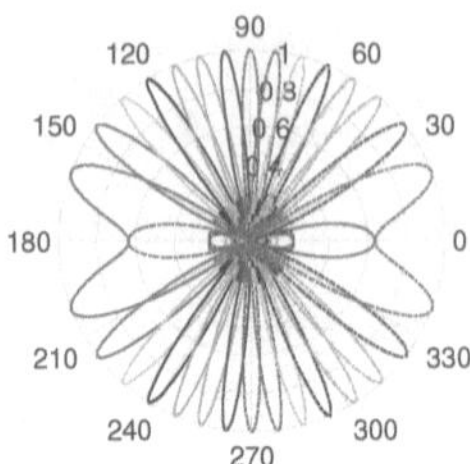

Figure 3.1: Beam patterns of all possible angular directions

3.2 Motivating Example

To elaborate, we present the following example: consider a point to point communication link between a TX with single antenna ($n_t = 1$) and RX with $n_r = 15$ antennas. Therefore, the vector of channel gains[1], $\boldsymbol{q}$, is a 15×1 vector, and its corresponding angular (virtual) channel, $\boldsymbol{q}^a$, is a vector of the same size and can be derived using the DFT matrix $\boldsymbol{U}_r$ as $\boldsymbol{q}^a = \boldsymbol{U}_r^H \boldsymbol{q}$ [52] (Recall Eq. (2.0.3)). Assume a single-path channel, i.e., the channel has only one cluster with a single path in it ($L = k = 1$). Let the path gain be denoted by α. For simplicity, assume $\alpha = 1$. Further, let us assume perfect sparsity such that the AoA is along one of the directions defined in the DFT matrix $\boldsymbol{U}_r$, i.e., the channel path will only contribute to one angular bin. Finally, let us also neglect the channel noise. Based on the channel description above, we get an angular channel vector of the form

$$\boldsymbol{q}^a = \begin{pmatrix} q_0^a & q_1^a & \cdots & q_{14}^a \end{pmatrix}^T ,\tag{3.2.1}$$

---

[1]Let all the channels have one single significant tap.

such that $q_i^a \in \{0, 1\}$ and the number of non-zero elements in $\boldsymbol{q}^a$ is 1. Any component of $\boldsymbol{q}^a$ can be measured using one of the beam patterns shown in Fig. 3.1.

Objective: Suppose the transmitter sends pilot symbols of the form $x=1$. Thus, the received vector $\boldsymbol{y}$ of size 15×1 can be obtained as

$$y = qx = q \iff y^a = q^a \tag{3.2.2}$$

where $\boldsymbol{y}^a$ is the received vector in the angular domain. So, with change of basis, we can think of $\boldsymbol{q}^a$ as a received sequence with just one non-zero component. To identify the position of this non-zero component, the receiver performs a sequence of channel measurements. Let y_{s_i} denote the ith measurement such that

$$y_{s_i} = \boldsymbol{w}_i^H \boldsymbol{y} = \boldsymbol{w}_i^H \boldsymbol{q}, \tag{3.2.3}$$

where $\boldsymbol{w}_i$ denotes the ith receive (rx-)combining vector. Our aim is to design channel measurements (i.e., $\boldsymbol{w_i}$'s) such that the correct AoA is identified using the minimum number of measurements.

Proposed Solution: We consider this non-zero component to be an anomaly to a normally all-zero 15-bin angular channel. Hence, the goal of identifying its position is analogous to finding the most likely 1-bit error pattern of a 15-bit codeword in a linear block code. Now, we need to identify an error correction code with codewords of length 15 and with 1-bit error correction capability [53]. Hence, we can use the

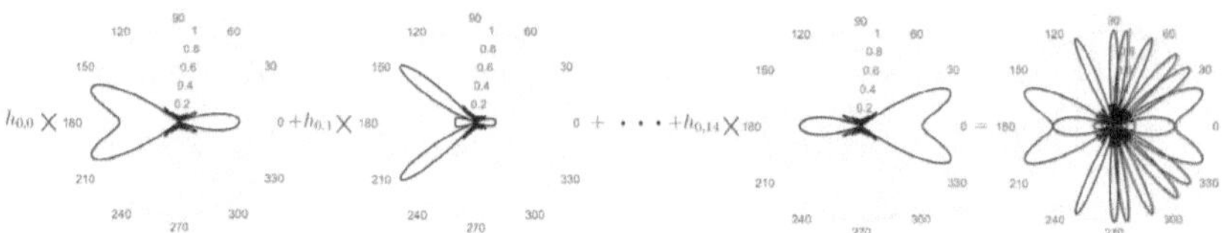

Figure 3.2: Beam pattern of receive combining vector $\boldsymbol{w_0}$

binary $(15, 11, 3)$ Hamming code with parity check matrix $\boldsymbol{H}$ of size 4×15, given by

$$\boldsymbol{H} = \begin{pmatrix} 1 & 0 & 0 & 0 & 1 & 0 & 0 & 1 & 1 & 0 & 1 & 0 & 1 & 1 & 1 \\ 0 & 1 & 0 & 0 & 1 & 1 & 0 & 1 & 0 & 1 & 1 & 1 & 1 & 0 & 0 \\ 0 & 0 & 1 & 0 & 0 & 1 & 1 & 0 & 1 & 0 & 1 & 1 & 1 & 1 & 0 \\ 0 & 0 & 0 & 1 & 0 & 0 & 1 & 1 & 0 & 1 & 0 & 1 & 1 & 1 & 1 \end{pmatrix}, \tag{3.2.4}$$

where $h_{i,j}$ represents the component at the intersection of row i and column j of $\boldsymbol{H}$. Using hard decision decoding of LBCs, error syndrome vectors of length 4 are obtained. Every possible syndrome vector maps to only one correctable error pattern[2]. Similarly, for channel estimation, several measurements should be performed at RX where each measurement mimics the behavior of a corresponding element in the error syndrome vector. Each measurement boils down to adding signals from a subset of the available 15 directions. Since each measurement can either include the direction of the incoming strong path of gain $\alpha = 1$ or no strong paths at all, then the elements of the channel syndrome vector are in $\{0, 1\}$.

For every measurement y_{s_i}, we design $\boldsymbol{w_i}$ based on the entries of the ith row of $\boldsymbol{H}$ such that: if $h_{i,j} = 1$, then we include the beam pattern that points to direction j in

[2]A correctable error pattern of a $(15, 11, 3)$ Hamming code is any 15×1 binary vector that contains only one '1' (at the error's position).

Table 3.1: Mapping of channel syndromes to angular channels

Channel Syndrome $\boldsymbol{y}_s^T$	Angular Channel $\boldsymbol{q}^{aT}$
[0 0 0 0]	[0 0 0 0 0 0 0 0 0 0 0 0 0 0 0]
[1 0 0 0]	[1 0 0 0 0 0 0 0 0 0 0 0 0 0 0]
[0 1 0 0]	[0 1 0 0 0 0 0 0 0 0 0 0 0 0 0]
[0 0 1 0]	[0 0 1 0 0 0 0 0 0 0 0 0 0 0 0]
[0 0 0 1]	[0 0 0 1 0 0 0 0 0 0 0 0 0 0 0]
[1 1 0 0]	[0 0 0 0 1 0 0 0 0 0 0 0 0 0 0]
[0 1 1 0]	[0 0 0 0 0 1 0 0 0 0 0 0 0 0 0]
[0 0 1 1]	[0 0 0 0 0 0 1 0 0 0 0 0 0 0 0]
[1 1 0 1]	[0 0 0 0 0 0 0 1 0 0 0 0 0 0 0]
[1 0 1 0]	[0 0 0 0 0 0 0 0 1 0 0 0 0 0 0]
[0 1 0 1]	[0 0 0 0 0 0 0 0 0 1 0 0 0 0 0]
[1 1 1 0]	[0 0 0 0 0 0 0 0 0 0 1 0 0 0 0]
[0 1 1 1]	[0 0 0 0 0 0 0 0 0 0 0 1 0 0 0]
[1 1 1 1]	[0 0 0 0 0 0 0 0 0 0 0 0 1 0 0]
[1 0 1 1]	[0 0 0 0 0 0 0 0 0 0 0 0 0 1 0]
[1 0 0 1]	[0 0 0 0 0 0 0 0 0 0 0 0 0 0 1]

$\boldsymbol{w}_i$. For example, the 0th row of $\boldsymbol{H}$ is given by [100010011010111]. Hence, $\boldsymbol{w}_0$ should include beam patterns pointing to the set of directions $\{0, 4, 7, 8, 10, 12, 13, 14\}$.

Fig. 3.2 illustrates this operation for $\boldsymbol{w}_0$. We can see that the resultant beam pattern of $\boldsymbol{w}_i$ combines signals coming from a set of selected directions dictated by the ith row of $\boldsymbol{H}$. We call the obtained measurement vector, $\boldsymbol{y}_s$, the *channel syndrome* which is analogous to error syndromes in hard decision decoding of LBCs. Then, a table that maps every possible channel syndrome to a unique corresponding channel can be constructed. Table 3.1 shows this mapping.

In this example, we are able to estimate the channel based on only 4 measurements as opposed to 15, which is the number of measurements with exhaustive search. Important aspects of our proposed method include the choice of codes, the design of precoding and rx-combining measurement vectors, the effect of variable gains and phases of different paths and the occurrence of measurement errors.

Remark 3.2.0.1 (Receiver Architecture). *Note that, to achieve beam patterns similar to the one shown in Fig. 3.2, the receiver architecture needs to be a bit different from those of classical analog/hybrid beamforming architectures. Specifically, in addition to low-noise amplifiers (LNA) typically placed at the output of each antenna, we will need to add controllable low-power amplifiers, as well. The resultant architecture is still quite simple (see Fig. 2.1). That is, besides the low-power amplifiers, the proposed architecture is similar to those of simple analog beamforming. Moreover, relatively low-resolution ADCs can be used which mitigates the high power consumption problem associated with high-resolution ADCs.*

Motivation for LBC-inspired approach: LBCs are designed to discover and correct a certain maximum number of errors in a codeword of a specified length. This objective is achieved by adding redundant *parity check* bits to the original information sequence. What makes our devised approach attractive is that the number of measurements needed for channel estimation can be shown to be equal to the number of parity bits of some corresponding code. Hence, we can control the estimation performance via appropriate code selection. In this work, we will propose a method to specify the number of necessary channel measurements as a function of the rate of the underlying code.

3.3   Problem Statement

Suppose a maximum number of k paths need to be discovered in the channel where $k \ll n_t, n_r$. Under the prefect sparsity assumption, $\boldsymbol{Q}^a$ has a maximum of k non-zero RX and TX angular bins. Our objective is to identify the angular positions at which channel paths exist and identify their path gain values using the **least possible number of measurements**. Let the number of measurements be m such that each measurement, $u_{s_{i,j}}$, is obtained using the precoder $\boldsymbol{f_j}$ and rx-combiner $\boldsymbol{w_i}$. Let the number of rx-combiners and precoders be m_r and m_t, respectively. Measurements take the form $u_{s_{i,j}} = [\boldsymbol{w_i^H Q f_j} s + \boldsymbol{w_i^H n}]_+$. Let $\mathcal{D}(\cdot)$ be a mapping function that takes in the measurements $\{u_{s_{i,j}}\}_{\forall i,j}$ as inputs and returns the estimated channel $\widehat{\boldsymbol{Q}}^a$. For each j, we stack the measurements $\{u_{s_{i,j}}\}_{\forall i}$ in a single (syndrome) vector such that $\boldsymbol{u_{s_j}} = [u_{s_{0,j}}\, u_{s_{1,j}} \ldots u_{s_{m_r-1,j}}]^T$. Our design variables are the precoding vectors $\boldsymbol{f_j}$, rx-combining vectors $\boldsymbol{w_i}$, the number of measurements m, the mapping function $\mathcal{D}()$, and the transmitted symbol power P.

In its essence, solving this problem boils down to finding the optimal set of measurements $\{u_{s_{i,j}}\}_{\forall i,j}$ and the mapping function $\mathcal{D}(\cdot)$ such that $\boldsymbol{Q}^a$ can be estimated using the minimum number of measurements. For ease of explanation, we first consider a channel with a single transmit antenna and n_r receive antennas. Therefore, no precoding is needed and the design of measurements is reduced to designing the rx-combining vectors $\boldsymbol{w_i}$. Recall that in the motivating example in Section 3.2, we dealt with a special case of $n_r \times 1$ channels where we sought to find the direction of arrival of a channel with a single path of known gain, $\alpha = 1$. In the general case, we should consider arbitrary path gains $\alpha \in \mathbb{C}$ and channels with multiple paths.

3.4   Beam Discovery

In this section, we present our proposed solution. As an initial step, we solve a simplified version of the problem where communication channels have a single transmit antenna and multiple receive antennas. Afterwards, we will build on it to provide the solution for general channels with multiple transmit and receive antennas.

3.4.1 Beam Detection using LBC-inspired approach

To identify the exact number of measurements and their corresponding design, we follow a decoding-like approach of LBC[3]. First, we need to find an LBC, C, that has an error correction capability e_n such that i) the maximum number of paths in the channel, k, is equal to e_n and ii) the length of its codewords n is equal to the number of antennas n_r (n_r is also the number of resolvable directions). The code C has a parity check matrix $\boldsymbol{H}$ which represents the link between channel decoding and beam detection problems. Binary codes deal with data and error sequences defined over the finite field $GF(2)$, i.e., addition and multiplication operations are defined over $GF(2)$ with binary inputs and outputs, i.e., 1's and 0's. However, mm-wave channel parameters are defined over the complex numbers field $\mathbb{C}$. Therefore, to account for arbitrary path gains, we should be able to extend this concept to $\mathbb{C}$.

Although $\boldsymbol{H}$ is defined over $GF(2)$, we interpret its '1' and '0' entries as real numbers. Then, similar to channel decoding, we seek to obtain a channel syndrome, $\boldsymbol{y_s}$, such that $(\boldsymbol{y_s})^T = (\boldsymbol{q}^a)^T \boldsymbol{H}^T \implies \boldsymbol{y_s} = \boldsymbol{H}\boldsymbol{q}^a$. This matrix multiplication can be realized using channel measurements such that each measurement gives one component in $\boldsymbol{y_s}$. Measurements $\{y_{s_i}\}_{\forall i}$ make up the components of the channel syndrome vector $\boldsymbol{y_s}$. Then, we need to find a mapping function $\mathcal{D}()$ that takes in the channel syndrome vector $\{\boldsymbol{y_s}\}$ as an input and returns the estimated channel $\widehat{\boldsymbol{q}}^a$. The position of each non-zero component in $\widehat{\boldsymbol{q}}^a$ identifies a path's AoA, and its value

---

[3]In channel coding, the convention is to use row vectors. Thus, let $\boldsymbol{x}$ and $\boldsymbol{c}$ be $1 \times o$ and $1 \times n$ binary row vectors that represent an information sequence and its corresponding codeword of an LBC, respectively. Also let $\boldsymbol{r} = \boldsymbol{c} + \boldsymbol{e}$ be a received sequence corrupted by $1 \times n$ error pattern $\boldsymbol{e}$. To decode $\boldsymbol{r}$, we calculate an error syndrome vector $\boldsymbol{s}$, of size $1 \times n - o$, such that $\boldsymbol{s} = \boldsymbol{r}\boldsymbol{H}^T$, where $\boldsymbol{H}$ is the parity check matrix of the used LBC. Then, a most likely error pattern $\hat{\boldsymbol{e}}$ can be uniquely identified by $\boldsymbol{s}$ using a look-up table called the *standard array*. Finally, the decoded codeword is obtained using $\hat{\boldsymbol{c}} = \boldsymbol{r} - \hat{\boldsymbol{e}}$. A decoding error occurs if the number of errors, identified using 1's in $\boldsymbol{e}$, is beyond the error correction capability of the used code, denoted by e_n. Note that in this context, all vectors, matrices and math operations are over $GF(2)$.

identifies its baseband path gain. Finally, for this to work, we need to show that such channel measurements provide one-to-one mapping to the channel. In other words, $\boldsymbol{y_s}$ must be a *sufficient statistic* for estimating the channel. In Section 3.4.3, we will show that our design results in the sufficient statistic we seek to achieve.

Remark 3.4.0.1 (Difference between $\boldsymbol{y_s}$ and $\boldsymbol{u_s}$). *Both $\boldsymbol{y_s}$ and $\boldsymbol{u_s}$ refer to vectors of measurement symbols, however, $\boldsymbol{u_s}$ is considered to be the noise corrupted and quantized version of $\boldsymbol{y_s}$. Specifically, $\boldsymbol{u_s} = [\boldsymbol{y_s} + \boldsymbol{w}^H \boldsymbol{n}]_+$ such that $\boldsymbol{w}^H \boldsymbol{n}$ is the measurement noise vector. While $\boldsymbol{u_s}$ is what we expect to observe, our design of measurements focuses on finding $\boldsymbol{y_s}$; an error-free symbol. Of course, errors degrade beam discovery performance. Thus, in Section 3.5, we will deal with the effect of measurement errors separately and present a solution that increases reliability of beam discovery. The separate treatment of measurement errors simplifies the design and provides a clear understanding of the nature of our solution.*

Remark 3.4.0.2 (Number of Measurements). *The solution we obtain is dependent on channel parameters, namely, the number of antennas and the sparsity level of the channel. That is, at a fixed sparsity level, i.e., fixed number of paths k, a larger number of antennas necessitates more channel measurements. In other other words, the high resolution realized by large n_r comes at a price of an increased number of measurements. Similarly, at fixed n_r, more channel paths require more measurements for correct channel estimation.*

3.4.2 Measurements Design

Recall that each component in $\boldsymbol{q}^a$ represents a resolvable angular direction at the receiver. Let each resolvable direction be given an identification number ($dir_{rx}\#i$). Also let $beam_{rx}\#i$ denote the beam pattern pointing to $dir_{rx}\#i$, i.e., a signal coming from $dir_{rx}\#i$ can be individually measured using $beam_{rx}\#i$ (similar to beam patterns in Fig. 3.1).

Now, using careful design of $\boldsymbol{w_i}$'s, we seek to obtain

$$\boldsymbol{y_s} = \left(y_{s_0}, y_{s_1}, \dots, y_{s_{m_r-1}} \right)^T = \boldsymbol{H}\boldsymbol{q^a}, \text{ where} \tag{3.4.1}$$

$$y_{s_i} = \boldsymbol{w}_i^H \boldsymbol{q} \quad , \forall\, 0 \le i \le m_r-1 \tag{3.4.2}$$

To achieve this, each rx-combining vector $\boldsymbol{w_i}$ is designed as a multi-armed beam, i.e., composed of several sub-beams similar to the beam pattern in Fig. 3.2. The sub-beams included in each $\boldsymbol{w_i}$ are identified by the ith row of the matrix $\boldsymbol{H}$. That is, only if $h_{i,j}$, the intersection of the ith row and j^{th} column, is $= 1$, do we include $beam_{rx}\#j$ as a sub-beam in $\boldsymbol{w_i}$ (also refer to our discussion in Section 3.2).

The design of rx-combining vectors is a crucial aspect of this work. As an initial step towards obtaining proper rx-combining vectors, we consider designing $\boldsymbol{w_i}$'s using linear summation of all analog beamformers that correspond to $beam_{rx}\#j$'s $\forall j : h_{i,j} = 1$. Let $\Omega_j = \cos(\phi_j) = \dfrac{j}{L_r}\ \forall j \in \{0, \dots, n_r-1\}$, such that $\boldsymbol{e_r}(\Omega_j)$ is the spatial signature of $beam_{rx}\#j$. Then, $\boldsymbol{w_i}$ can be designed as

$$\boldsymbol{w_i} = \sum_{j=0}^{n_r-1} \mathbb{1}_{\{h_{i,j}=1\}} \boldsymbol{e_r}(\Omega_j) \tag{3.4.3}$$

3.4.3 Sufficient Statistic

We will show in this section that each channel syndrome can only be mapped to a single *measurable channel*. A measurable channel in this context refers to $n_r \times 1$ channels with k non-zero components such that $k \le e_n$, where e_n is the error correction capability of the underlying code C and $n_r=n$ is its CWs length. Let $\mathcal{Q}^a$ be the set of all measurable channels:

$$\mathcal{Q}^a \triangleq \{q^a \in \mathbb{C}^{n_r} : |q_i^a{:}q_i^a{\neq}0| \leq e_n\}. \tag{3.4.4}$$

Since each measurement combines signals coming from multiple directions, each element in the channel syndrome vector is a linear combination of a subset of the available paths. In other words, each measurement has the possibility that one or more paths are included in it. This setting is rather challenging. To understand why, consider a channel that has two paths with gains $\alpha_1, \alpha_2 \in \mathbb{C}$. Suppose that α_1 and α_2 are of equal magnitudes but are out-of-phase (i.e., phase shift $= 180°$). Hence, if signals coming from both paths are combined in a single measurement, the resultant value is 0 which is similar to the result we get if no paths exist in the measured directions. Also each channel measurement can be a result of endless possibilities for the combined path gain values. So, a natural question to ask is: does this ambiguity cause measurement errors? The direct answer to this question is: **No**. In the sequel we will show that the resulting channel syndrome, i.e., the combination of all channel measurements, is sufficient to correctly estimate the channel.

First, recall our discussion in Footnote 3. Then, consider all *single-bit error patterns* $e^{(i)}$ of a code C, with maximum number of correctable errors $=e_n$, such that

$$e_j^{(i)} = \begin{cases} 1, & j = i \\ 0, & j \neq i \end{cases} \tag{3.4.5}$$

where $e_j^{(i)}$ is the jth component of $e^{(i)}$. Also let $s^{(i)}$ be the corresponding error syndrome of $e^{(i)}$. Recall that $s^{(i)}=e^{(i)}H^T$. Hence, we can see that $s^{(i)}$ is exactly the ith row of H^T, i.e., i^{th} column of H. Let $\mathcal{E}_C$ denote the set of correctable error patterns of the code C :

$$\mathcal{E}_C \triangleq \left\{ e \in \{0,1\}^n : e = \sum_{i=1}^{n} \omega_i e^{(i)}, \omega_i \in \{0,1\} : |\omega_i : \omega_i = 1| \leq e_n \right\}. \tag{3.4.6}$$

Now, we can write any correctable error pattern $e \in \mathcal{E}_C$ as a linear combination of all single-bit error patterns over the finite field $GF(2)$ such that

$$e = \omega_1 e^{(1)} + \omega_2 e^{(2)} + \cdots + \omega_n e^{(n)} \tag{3.4.7}$$

and its corresponding error syndrome is

$$s = \omega_1 s^{(1)} + \omega_2 s^{(2)} + \cdots + \omega_n s^{(n)} \tag{3.4.8}$$

Lemma 3.4.1. *For an error pattern e_p with number of bit errors identical to e_n, its syndrome s_p is a linear combination of e_n linearly independent vectors $s^{(i)}$.*

Proof. We are going to prove this lemma by contradiction. First, assume that s_p is a linear combination of e_n linearly **dependent** vectors $s^{(i)}$ over $GF(2)$. Therefore, there exists another error syndrome s_p^* composed of only linear combination of independent vectors $s^{(i)}$ such that $s_p = s_p^*$. Therefore, there exists another error patter e_p^* with number of errors strictly less than e_n such that its syndrome $s_p^* = s_p$. Since e_p^* has a number of errors less than e_n, then it is a correctable error pattern, and since all error syndromes of correctable error patterns are different, then s_p^* should be $\neq s_p$. Hence, we arrive at a contradiction. $\square$

It is also easy to see that if e_{p_1} and e_{p_2} are two different correctable error patterns, then their error syndromes s_{p_1} and s_{p_2} are composed of a linear combination of different sets of single-bit error syndromes $s^{(i)}$.

Lemma 3.4.2. *Any $n-$dimensional linearly independent vectors over $GF(2)$, are also linearly independent over $\mathbb{C}^n$.*

Proof. Let $\boldsymbol{v}_1, \ldots, \boldsymbol{v}_m$ be a set of $n-$dimensional vectors defined over $GF(2)$. The vectors $\boldsymbol{v}_i$ can be made the columns of an $n \times m$ matrix $\boldsymbol{\Psi}$. Since all $\boldsymbol{v}_i$'s are linearly independent over $GF(2)$, then $\boldsymbol{\Psi}$ is a left-invertible matrix. Therefore, there exists a non-zero (modulo 2) $m \times m$ minor of $\boldsymbol{\Psi}$. Now, suppose the entries in $\boldsymbol{\Psi}$ are interpreted as real numbers. Therefore, $\boldsymbol{\Psi}$, now taken over $\mathbb{R}$, has an $m \times m$ sub-matrix whose determinant is non-zero, which proves that it is invertible. Therefore, the vectors $\boldsymbol{v}_i$'s, i.e., columns of $\boldsymbol{\Psi}$, are linearly independent over $\mathbb{R}$ which, using the same argument, can also be shown to be linearly independent over $\mathbb{C}$. $\qquad\square$

Suppose that entries of $\boldsymbol{H}$ and $\boldsymbol{e}^{(i)}$ are interpreted as real numbers, then we can write the channel $\boldsymbol{q}^a$ as

$$(\boldsymbol{q}^a)^T = \alpha_1 \boldsymbol{e}^{(1)} + \alpha_2 \boldsymbol{e}^{(2)} + \cdots + \alpha_n \boldsymbol{e}^{(n)} \tag{3.4.9}$$

where $\alpha_i \in \mathbb{C}$ and $\sum_{i=1}^{n} \mathbb{1}_{\{\alpha_i \neq 0\}} \leq e_n$. Therefore, each channel syndrome $(\boldsymbol{y}_s)^T = (\boldsymbol{q}^a)^T \boldsymbol{H}^T \implies \boldsymbol{y}_s = \boldsymbol{H}\boldsymbol{q}^a$ is a linear combination of independent vectors in $\mathbb{C}^{n-o}$ (columns of $\boldsymbol{H}$). Therefore, all possible measurable channels yield unique channel syndromes which implies that they are sufficient for the channel estimation problem.

3.4.4 Mapping Function $\mathcal{D}(\cdot)$

After showing that each measurable channel can be mapped to a unique channel syndrome, we need to find this mapping function, i.e., $\mathcal{D} : \boldsymbol{y}_s \rightarrow \widehat{\boldsymbol{q}}^a$, where $\widehat{\boldsymbol{q}}^a$ denotes the estimated channel. We propose two different approaches to find $\mathcal{D}(\cdot)$.

Look-up Table Method

Similar to hard decision decoding where a look-up table is constructed that maps error syndromes to their corresponding error patterns, we can construct a look-up table that indicates which channel corresponds to an obtained channel syndrome. The number of table entries depend on the employed ADC resolution and are based on error-free channel syndromes $\boldsymbol{y_s}$. The mapping between the actual error-corrupted syndrome $\boldsymbol{u_s}$ and $\boldsymbol{q^a}$ is obtained using l^2- norm minimization where $\mathcal{D}()$ returns the channel whose corresponding $\boldsymbol{y_s}$ has the smallest distance to $\boldsymbol{u_s}$. The l^2 distance function $\delta(\cdot,\cdot)$ is given by

$$\delta(\boldsymbol{y_s}, \boldsymbol{u_s}) = \|\boldsymbol{y_s} - \boldsymbol{u_s}\|_2 = \sqrt{\sum_{i=0}^{m-1} |y_{s_i} - u_{s_i}|^2}. \tag{3.4.10}$$

Further details of the table construction can be found in [54].

Search Method

Recall that $\boldsymbol{y_s} = \boldsymbol{H}\boldsymbol{q^a}$ (Eq. (3.4.1)), and let the parity check matrix $\boldsymbol{H}$ be represented using its columns $\boldsymbol{h_i}$ as:

$$\boldsymbol{H} = \begin{pmatrix} \boldsymbol{h_1} & \boldsymbol{h_2} & \cdots & \boldsymbol{h_{n_r}} \end{pmatrix}, \tag{3.4.11}$$

where $\boldsymbol{h_i}$ is the ith column of $\boldsymbol{H}$. Thus, we can write $\boldsymbol{y_s}$ as:

$$\boldsymbol{y_s} = q_1^a \boldsymbol{h_1} + q_2^a \boldsymbol{h_2} + \cdots + q_{n_r}^a \boldsymbol{h_{n_r}}, \tag{3.4.12}$$

where q_i^a is the ith component of $\boldsymbol{q^a}$. Note that $\boldsymbol{q^a}$ is $k-$sparse, i.e., we have no more than k non-zero components q_i^a. Let the indices of the non-zero components be

$x_1, x_2, \ldots, x_k$, hence, $\boldsymbol{y_s}$ can succinctly be written as:

$$\boldsymbol{y_s} = q^a_{x_1} \boldsymbol{h_{x_1}} + q^a_{x_2} \boldsymbol{h_{x_2}} + \cdots + q^a_{x_k} \boldsymbol{h_{x_k}}. \tag{3.4.13}$$

Then, we can write Eq. (3.4.13) in matrix form as:

$$\boldsymbol{y_s} = \boldsymbol{C} \boldsymbol{q^a_c}, \quad \text{where} \tag{3.4.14}$$

$$\boldsymbol{C} \triangleq \begin{pmatrix} \boldsymbol{h_{x_1}} & \boldsymbol{h_{x_2}} & \cdots & \boldsymbol{h_{x_k}} \end{pmatrix} \tag{3.4.15}$$

and $\boldsymbol{q^a_c} = \begin{pmatrix} q^a_{x_1} & q^a_{x_2} & \cdots q^a_{x_k} \end{pmatrix}^T$ is a shortened version of $\boldsymbol{q^a}$ that only has k dimensions. Also $\boldsymbol{C}$ is an $m \times k$ matrix of rank k, since $k < m$, and $\boldsymbol{h_{x_i}}$'s are linearly independent columns of $\boldsymbol{C}$ (recall our discussion in Section 3.4.3). Therefore, $\boldsymbol{C}$ has a left Moore-Penrose inverse (pseudo inverse), $\boldsymbol{C^+} = (\boldsymbol{C^T C})^{-1} \boldsymbol{C^T}$ where $\boldsymbol{C^+ C} = \boldsymbol{I}$ of size $k \times k$. Thus, if we have knowledge of $\boldsymbol{C}$, we can then find $\boldsymbol{q^a_c}$ as:

$$\boldsymbol{q^a_c} = \boldsymbol{C^+} \boldsymbol{y_s}. \tag{3.4.16}$$

The problem we need to solve is obtaining the matrix $\boldsymbol{C}$. We can solve this problem using an exhaustive search method which can be explained as follows:

(i) Candidate matrices $\boldsymbol{C_j}$ are generated by choosing different k combinations of columns of $\boldsymbol{H}$ where $1 \leq j \leq \binom{n_r}{k}$.

(ii) Find $\boldsymbol{q^a_{c_j}} = \boldsymbol{C^+_j} \boldsymbol{y_s} = \boldsymbol{C^+_j} \boldsymbol{C} \boldsymbol{q^a_c}$. Note that at this step, we obtain a vector $\boldsymbol{q^a_{c_j}}$ identical to $\boldsymbol{q^a_c}$ if and only if $\boldsymbol{C^+_j C} = \boldsymbol{I} \Leftrightarrow \boldsymbol{C_j} = \boldsymbol{C}$.

(iii) Let $\boldsymbol{\beta_j}$ be such that

$$\boldsymbol{\beta_j} = \boldsymbol{C_j} \boldsymbol{q^a_{c_j}} = \boldsymbol{C_j} \boldsymbol{C^+_j} \boldsymbol{y_s}, \tag{3.4.17}$$

Hence, if the correct choice $C_j = C$ is made, then

$$\beta_j = C_j C_j^+ C q_c^a = y_s,$$

else, if $C_j \neq C$, then[4]

$$\beta_j = C_j C_j^+ C q_c^a \neq y_s$$

Hence, if $\beta_{j^*} = y_s$, we declare its corresponding matrix C_{j^*} the true matrix C defined in Eq. (3.4.15) which satisfies Eq. (3.4.14). Also, we have that $q_c^a = q_{c_{j^*}}^a$. Since, identifying C is equivalent to identifying the indexes $x_1, \ldots, x_k$. Thus, we found the angular channel q^a which is all zeros except - potentially[5] - for the components $q_{x_1}^a, \ldots, q_{x_k}^a$.

The previous discussion dealt with an idealized version of the measurements (i.e., y_s), however, in practice, we observe u_s as an error-corrupted version of y_s. Define z_s to be the error vector that captures the effect of both channel noise and quantization error which satisfies

$$u_s = y_s + z_s. \tag{3.4.18}$$

Suppose that we know the matrix C for which we have

$$u_s = C q_c^a + z_s, \tag{3.4.19}$$

---

[4]Since C_j^+ is the left pseudo-inverse of C_j, and since C_j is not a square matrix, then $C_j C_j^+ \neq I = C_j^+ C_j \implies C_j C_j^+ C \neq C$

[5]This means that if the number of paths is less than k, then some $q_{x_i}^a$'s might have zero values as well.

then, we can find $C^+ u_s$ (compare to Eq. (3.4.16)) as follows

$$C^+ u_s = C^+ C q_c^a + C^+ z_s = q_c^a + C^+ z_s,$$

to be a noise-corrupted version of q_c^a.

Now, to find an estimate $\hat{q}^a$ of q^a, we follow a very similar procedure to the one described before as follows:

(i) Matrices C_j are generated similar to the 1st step before.

(ii) Define E_j to be the difference between C and C_j where

$$C = C_j + E_j. \tag{3.4.20}$$

That is, $E_j = 0$ (all zero matrix) $\Leftrightarrow C_j = C$.

(iii) Find $q_{c_j}^a$ such that

$$q_{c_j}^a = C_j^+ u_s = q_c^a + C_j^+ (E_j q_c^a + z_s). \tag{3.4.21}$$

Unlike the 2nd step of the no-error case, $q_{c_j}^a$ will not be identical to the true q_c^a with probability 1, since z_s is not identical to 0 with probability 1 (z_s is the difference between continuous and discrete quantities).

(iv) Let β_j be such that

$$\beta_j = C_j q_{c_j}^a = C_j \left(q_c^a + C_j^+ \left(E_j q_c^a + z_s \right) \right) \tag{3.4.22}$$

$$= \begin{cases} y_s + C_j C_j^+ z_s & , C = C_j \\ C_j q_c^a + C_j C_j^+ \left(E_j q_c^a + z_s \right) & , C \neq C_j \end{cases} \tag{3.4.23}$$

Then find j^* such that

$$j^* = \arg\min_j \|\boldsymbol{\beta}_j - \boldsymbol{u_s}\|, \tag{3.4.24}$$

where $\boldsymbol{\beta}_j - \boldsymbol{u_s}$ is given by

$$\boldsymbol{\beta}_j - \boldsymbol{u_s} = \boldsymbol{C}_j \boldsymbol{q_c^a} - \boldsymbol{y_s} + \boldsymbol{C}_j \boldsymbol{C}_j^+ \boldsymbol{E}_j \boldsymbol{q_c^a} + \left(\boldsymbol{C}_j \boldsymbol{C}_j^+ - \boldsymbol{I}\right) \boldsymbol{z_s} \tag{3.4.25}$$

which at $\boldsymbol{C} = \boldsymbol{C}_{j^*}$ is further reduced to

$$\boldsymbol{\beta}_{j^*} - \boldsymbol{u_s} = \left(\boldsymbol{C}_j \boldsymbol{C}_j^+ - \boldsymbol{I}\right) \boldsymbol{z_s} \tag{3.4.26}$$

3.4.5 Multiple Transmit and Receive Antennas

So far, we have considered channels with single transmit antennas and shown how to perform beam discovery at RX. To extend our approach to a general setting, we consider channels with n_t antennas at TX, and n_r antennas at RX. Thus, instead of the TX just sending signals omnidirectionally, now it can perform highly directional transmission. Recall that the RX is able to perform channel measurements using multi-armed beams. Similarly, the TX can send signals using multi-armed beams to simultaneously focus on multiple directions using precoding vectors $\boldsymbol{f}_j$.

The design of precoding vectors can also be obtained using an LBC approach. Similar to the method of designing rx-combining vectors $\boldsymbol{w}_i$, we look for an LBC, C_t, that has CWs of length n_t and can correct for $e_n = k$ errors. Let the parity check matrix of C_t be $\boldsymbol{H}_t$, using which, we will design the precoding vectors $\boldsymbol{f}_j$. Let $beam_{tx}\#i$ denote the ith TX beam which points to TX direction $dir_{tx}\ \#i$. Then, just as before, we envisage $\boldsymbol{H}_t$ as an array whose columns are associated with resolvable TX directions such that: i) its jth column corresponds to $dir_{tx}\#j$, and ii) its ith

row corresponds to the ith measurement. We note that no actual measurements are performed at TX; we use the word *measurement* to refer to precoding, consistent with the case of RX. That is, the ith TX measurement is actually the ith precoder $\boldsymbol{f}_i$. Thereby, we design the ith precoder as a multi-armed TX beam such that, only if $h_{i,j}$, the intersection of the ith row and j^{th} columns of $\boldsymbol{H}_t$, is $= 1$, do we include sub-beam $beam_{tx}\#j$ in $\boldsymbol{f}_i$. Each TX measurement provides a component in a TX channel syndrome vector $\boldsymbol{y}_s^{TX}$. The total number of TX measurements (i.e., precoding vectors), denoted by m_t, is equal to the number of parity check bits of the code C_t. That is, $m_t = n_t - o_t$, where o_t is the length of C_t's information sequences. To obtain AoDs of strong paths at TX, we define the function $\mathcal{D}_t()$ as the mapping function between all possible TX channel syndromes and their corresponding angular channels denoted by $\boldsymbol{q}^{aTX}$. Note that, for every $dir_{rx}\#i$, there exists a corresponding $\boldsymbol{q}^{aTX(i)}$ which represents the ith row of $\boldsymbol{Q}^a$. Also, since the maximum number of paths is k, then, the number of non-zero vectors $\boldsymbol{q}^{aTX(i)}$ is $\leq k$.

To see the whole picture, assume that a code C_r, with CWs of length n_r, is an LBC code associated with beam discovery at RX side. Let the number of RX measurements, i.e., the number of rx-combining vectors, be m_r such that $m_r = n_r - o_r$, where o_r is the length of information sequences of C_r. Also let $\mathcal{D}_r()$ be the mapping function between RX channel syndromes and its corresponding angular channel. Under this setting, the beam discovery problem is performed as follows: i) The TX starts starts sending its training sequence using the precoder $\boldsymbol{f}_j, \forall j \in \{0, \ldots, m_t-1\}$. ii) The RX performs m_r channel measurements while $\boldsymbol{f}_j$ is being used at TX and obtains a channel syndrome $\boldsymbol{y}_{s_j}$. iii) Based on $\boldsymbol{y}_{s_j}$, the RX obtains a corresponding channel, $\boldsymbol{q}^{a(j)}$ with path components $\{q_p^{a(j)}\}_{\forall p \in \{1,\ldots,n_r\}}$. Notice that $\boldsymbol{q}^{a(j)}$'s do not necessarily represent individual path gains, but rather, combinations of paths accumulating at a single $dir_{rx}\#$. Therefore, there exists a resemblance to channel syndromes which we exploit.

Algorithm 3.1: Beam discovery of multiple TX/RX antennas.

> **input** : $\{\boldsymbol{w}_i\}_{\forall i \in \{1,\ldots,m_r\}}$, $\{\boldsymbol{f}_j\}_{,\forall j \in \{1,\ldots,m_t\}}$, $\mathcal{D}_t() : \boldsymbol{y}_s \to \widehat{\boldsymbol{q}}^a$,
> $\qquad\quad \mathcal{D}_r() : \boldsymbol{y}_s^{TX} \to \hat{\boldsymbol{q}}^{a^{TX}}$
> **output:** $\{\boldsymbol{y}_{s_i}\}_{\forall i \in \{1,\ldots,m_t\}}$

1 **begin**

2 $\quad$ $j = 0$;

3 $\quad$ **while** $j < m_t$ **do**

4 $\quad\quad$ $i = 0$;

5 $\quad\quad$ **while** $i < m_r$ **do**

6 $\quad\quad\quad$ $y_{s_{i,j}} = \boldsymbol{w}_i^H \boldsymbol{Q} \boldsymbol{f}_j s + \boldsymbol{w}_i^H \boldsymbol{n}$; $\qquad\qquad$ // channel measurement

7 $\quad\quad\quad$ $i \leftarrow i + 1$

8 $\quad\quad$ $\boldsymbol{y}_{s_j} \leftarrow \{y_{s_{i,j}}\}_{\forall i \in \{1,\ldots,m_r\}}$; $\qquad$ // construct channel syndrome $\boldsymbol{y}_{s_j}$

$\qquad\quad$ /* find corresponding channel $\boldsymbol{q}^{a(j)} = [q_1^{a(j)}, q_2^{a(j)}, \ldots, q_{n_r}^{a\ (j)}]^T$ */

9 $\quad\quad$ $\boldsymbol{q}^{a(j)} \leftarrow \mathcal{D}_r(\boldsymbol{y}_{s_j})$;

10 $\quad\quad$ **for** $p \leftarrow 1$ **to** n_r **do**

$\qquad\quad$ /* construct TX channel syndromes $\boldsymbol{y}_s^{TX(p)}$, where

$\qquad\qquad \boldsymbol{y}_s^{TX(p)} = [y_{s_1}^{TX(p)}, y_{s_2}^{TX(p)}, \ldots, y_{s_{m_t}}^{TX(p)}]^T$ $\qquad\qquad$ */

11 $\quad\quad\quad$ $y_{s_j}^{TX(p)} \leftarrow q_p^{a(j)}$

12 $\quad\quad$ $j \leftarrow j + 1$;

13 $\quad$ **for** $p \leftarrow 1$ **to** n_r **do**

14 $\quad\quad$ $\boldsymbol{q}^{aTX(p)} \leftarrow \mathcal{D}_t(\boldsymbol{y}_s^{TX(p)})$

15 $\quad$ $\widehat{\boldsymbol{Q}}^a = \begin{pmatrix} \boldsymbol{q}^{aTX(1)} & \boldsymbol{q}^{aTX(2)} & \ldots & \boldsymbol{q}^{aTX(n_r)} \end{pmatrix}^T$

---

iv) We construct a set of n_r TX channel syndromes, $\boldsymbol{y}_s^{TX(p)}$ where their j^{th} component $y_{s_j}^{TX(p)} = q_p^{a(j)}$, i.e., $[\boldsymbol{y}_s^{TX(1)}, \boldsymbol{y}_s^{TX(2)}, \ldots, \boldsymbol{y}_s^{TX(n_r)}] = [\boldsymbol{q}^{a(1)}, \boldsymbol{q}^{a(2)}, \ldots, \boldsymbol{q}^{a(m_t)}]^T$. v) Finally, we find the angular TX channel for every $dir_{rx} \#p$, i.e., p^{th} row of $\boldsymbol{Q}^a$, using the mapping function $\boldsymbol{q}^{aTX(p)} = \mathcal{D}_t(\boldsymbol{y}_s^{TX(p)})$. Notice that, since no more than $k \ll n_r$ paths exist, and since $\boldsymbol{0}$ channels correspond to $\boldsymbol{0}$ channel syndromes, we only need to apply $\mathcal{D}_t()$ a maximum of k times -unless measurement error occurs. This whole process is highlighted in Algorithm 3.1.

Remark 3.4.0.3. *The estimated channel* $\widehat{\boldsymbol{Q}}^a$ *may contain more than k non-zero* *components. The reason is that the receiver obtains a channel $\boldsymbol{q}^{a(j)}$ for every precoder $\boldsymbol{f}_j$ which may contain erroneous component estimates. Incorrect estimates occur as a result of measurement errors which happen due to i) channel noise, ii) quantization error. Now every $\boldsymbol{q}^{a(j)}$ may contain a maximum of k non-zero components, however, some of which may be due to measurement errors. Afterwards, potentially noise-corrupted $\{\boldsymbol{q}^{a(j)}\}_{\forall j \in \{1,...,n_r\}}$ are used to obtain TX channel syndromes as shown in Algorithm 3.1. That is, for every $dir_{rx}\#i$ we obtain a TX channel syndrome to identify the corresponding $dir_{tx}\#j$'s that have strong components. Thus, we may obtain a maximum of k non-zero components per $dir_{rx}\#i$.*

3.5　Error Correction

So far, the main focus of our work has been finding the most efficient way for beam discovery under the channel sparsity assumption. While doing so, we did not really have special treatment to deal with measurement errors. In fact, with no measurement errors, our proposed solution can estimate the channel matrix perfectly. However, the presence of channel noise and quantization degrades the beam discovery (channel estimation) performance. To combat the effect of such imperfections, we focus our attention on answering the following question: ***Can we trade efficiency for performance?*** By *efficiency* we refer to the reduced number of measurements. So, in other words, we need to study whether increasing the number of channel measurements — by essentially adding redundancy — would improve the beam detection performance. The answer to this is: **Yes**. In the sequel we will present a method that allows for increasing the number of measurements and trades it for higher reliability.

The very concept of adding redundant information to combat noisy observations is the foundation of channel coding. Hence, it is appealing to use channel coding ideas to achieve more reliable beam discovery. For simplicity we again present our proposed solution for the simple setting of one transmit antenna and multiple receive antennas. The general multiple transmit and receive antennas setting can be dealt with in the same fashion described in Section 3.4.5.

Recall that a received symbol u_s is given by Eq. (2.0.12) as $u_s=[y_s + \boldsymbol{w}^H\boldsymbol{n}]_+$ where $y_s=\boldsymbol{w}^H\boldsymbol{Q}\boldsymbol{f}s$ is the error-free measurement symbol. We write $u_s=y_s + z_s$ where z_s is the measurement error (Eq. (3.4.18)). Also recall that, for $\boldsymbol{f}=1$ (one transmit antenna), and $\boldsymbol{w_i}$, we form the channel syndrome vector $\boldsymbol{u_s}=[u_{s_0}\, u_{s_1}\, \cdots\, u_{s_{m-1}}]^T$ such that $u_{s_i}=\boldsymbol{w}_i^H\boldsymbol{q}s+z_{s_i}$ where $\boldsymbol{q}$ is the $n_r\times1$ channel vector. Equivalently, we have that $\boldsymbol{u_s}=\boldsymbol{H}\boldsymbol{q}^a+\boldsymbol{z_s}$ where $\boldsymbol{z_s}$ is formed by stacking $\{z_{s_i}\}_{\forall i=0,\ldots,m-1}$. Recall that this is exactly Eq. (3.4.1) but with the noise terms added.

In fact, we can perceive the channel syndrome $\boldsymbol{y_s}$ as raw information sequence that need to be transmitted over a noisy channel, and $\boldsymbol{u_s}$ is the noise-corrupted received sequence. The syndrome, $\boldsymbol{y_s}$, is a vector that lies in an $m-$dimensional vector space. By exploiting channel codes, we can map $\boldsymbol{y_s}$ to longer sequences $\boldsymbol{y_s^\nu}$ (encoded channel syndrome) that lie in an $m-$dimensional subspace of an m_c-dimensional vector space. The longer sequences $\boldsymbol{y_s^\nu}$ should have increased distance which allows for higher resilience against measurement errors. Hence, $\boldsymbol{u_s}$ can now be written as $\boldsymbol{u_s} = \boldsymbol{y_s^\nu} + \boldsymbol{z_s}$. Our goal is to design $\boldsymbol{y_s^\nu}$. Once we achieve that, the rest of the problem can be tackled as discussed in section 3.4.

Towards that end, let us use an error correction code C_c, with generator matrix $\boldsymbol{G_c}$ and error correction capability e_c. Note that we use the subscript c to refer to *correction*. The size of $\boldsymbol{G_c}$ is $m\times m_c$. Thus, the encoded channel syndromes can be represented as $\boldsymbol{y_s^\nu} = \boldsymbol{G_c^T}\boldsymbol{y_s}$, where $\boldsymbol{y_s}$ and $\boldsymbol{y_s^\nu}$ are of sizes $m\times1$ and $m_c\times1$, respectively. Thus, $\boldsymbol{y_s^\nu}$ can be written as $\boldsymbol{y_s^\nu} = \boldsymbol{G_c^T}\boldsymbol{H}\boldsymbol{q}^a$. Then, similar to Eqn. (3.4.1) we want to use the matrix $\boldsymbol{G_c^T}\boldsymbol{H}$ to design $\boldsymbol{y_s^\nu}$. However, the problem here is that this matrix in not necessarily a binary matrix (i.e., with elements of $'1's$ and $'0's$). Hence, let us denote by $\boldsymbol{H}^\nu$, the matrix $\boldsymbol{G}_c^T \boldsymbol{H}$ (mod 2) and use it to design $\boldsymbol{y}_s^\nu$ such that

$$\boldsymbol{y}_s^\nu = \boldsymbol{H}^\nu \boldsymbol{q}^a. \tag{3.5.1}$$

In other words, $\boldsymbol{H}^\nu = \boldsymbol{G}_c^T \boldsymbol{H}$ is the matrix product over $GF(2)$. Therefore, instead of designing the channel measurements based on $\boldsymbol{H}$, we propose to design them based on $\boldsymbol{H}^\nu$ with that being the only difference to the design proposed earlier.

At this point, it remains to show that the new measurements design still provides a one-to-one mapping to every angular channel (i.e., if $\boldsymbol{q}_1^a \neq \boldsymbol{q}_2^a$, then their corresponding channel syndromes $\boldsymbol{y}_{s1}^\nu \neq \boldsymbol{y}_{s2}^\nu$). Furthermore, we will show that the new design provides a better resilience to measurement errors. That is, we will show that if $\boldsymbol{q}_1^a \neq \boldsymbol{q}_2^a$, then $\delta(\boldsymbol{y}_{s1}, \boldsymbol{y}_{s2}) \leq \delta(\boldsymbol{y}_{s1}^\nu, \boldsymbol{y}_{s2}^\nu)$, where $\delta(\cdot, \cdot)$ is defined as in Eq. (3.4.10).

3.5.1 Sufficient Statistic

We start off by showing that the new measurements provide a sufficient statistic for beam discovery. We will follow a similar approach to that of Section 3.4.3. Specifically, we will first consider error patterns, matrices, and operators over the finite field $GF(2)$. Afterwards, we will extend those concepts to the complex field where all channel matrices and measurements lie.

Let us consider a code C, with codewords of length n and error correction capability e_n. The parity check and generator matrices of C are given by $\boldsymbol{H}$ and $\boldsymbol{G}$, respectively. The error syndromes of C are given by $\boldsymbol{s} = \boldsymbol{r}\boldsymbol{H}^T = \boldsymbol{e}\boldsymbol{H}^T$, where $\boldsymbol{r}$ is the received sequence and e is the error pattern corrupting the transmitted codeword $\boldsymbol{c}$ (recall Footnote 3). Now suppose we encode $\boldsymbol{s}$ using another error correction code C_c. The parity check and generator matrices of C_c are given by $\boldsymbol{H_c}$ and $\boldsymbol{G_c}$, respectively.

The encoded syndromes $\boldsymbol{s}^\nu$ are given as

$$\boldsymbol{s}^\nu \overset{(a)}{=} \boldsymbol{s}\boldsymbol{G}_c \overset{(b)}{=} \boldsymbol{e}\boldsymbol{H}^T\boldsymbol{G}_c \overset{(c)}{=} \boldsymbol{e}\boldsymbol{H}^{\nu T}, \tag{3.5.2}$$

Consider all single bit error patterns $\boldsymbol{e}^{(i)}$ as defined in Eq. (3.4.5). Let the encoded syndrome that corresponds to $\boldsymbol{e}^{(i)}$ be $\boldsymbol{s}^{\nu\,(i)} = \boldsymbol{e}^{(i)}\boldsymbol{H}^{\nu T}$. Thus, $\boldsymbol{s}^{\nu\,(i)}$ is exactly the ith row of $\boldsymbol{H}^{\nu T}$, i.e., i^{th} column of $\boldsymbol{H}^\nu$.

Lemma 3.5.1. *For any error sequence $\boldsymbol{e_p}$ with number of bit errors identical to e_n, its encoded syndrome $\boldsymbol{s}_p^\nu$ is a linear combination of e_n linearly independent vectors $\boldsymbol{s}^{\nu\,(i)}$.*

The proof of this lemma is similar to that of Lemma 3.4.1, and hence, is omitted here (see [54] for proof).

Lemma 3.5.1 allows us to use the result of Lemma 3.4.2 which states that if we have a collection, $\left\{\boldsymbol{s}^{\nu\,(i)}\right\}_{i=x_1}^{x_{e_n}}$, of linearly independent vectors over $GF(2)$. Then, if their $'1'$ and $'0'$ entries are interpreted as real numbers, then they are also linearly independent over $\mathbb{C}$.

Let us interpret the elements of $\boldsymbol{H}^\nu$ and $\boldsymbol{e}^{(i)}$ as real numbers. Then, we can write the channel $\boldsymbol{q}^a$ as

$$(\boldsymbol{q}^a)^T = \alpha_1\boldsymbol{e}^{(1)} + \alpha_2\boldsymbol{e}^{(2)} + \cdots + \alpha_n\boldsymbol{e}^{(n)} \tag{3.5.3}$$

where $\alpha_i\in\mathbb{C}$ and $\sum_{i=1}^{n}\mathbb{1}_{\{\alpha_i\neq 0\}}\leq e_n$. Therefore, each encoded channel syndrome $(\boldsymbol{y}_s^\nu)^T = (\boldsymbol{q}^a)^T\boldsymbol{H}^{\nu T} \implies \boldsymbol{y}_s^\nu = \boldsymbol{H}^\nu\boldsymbol{q}^a$ is a linear combination of independent vectors in $\mathbb{C}^{m_c}$ (columns of $\boldsymbol{H}^\nu$). Therefore, for all measurable channels $\boldsymbol{q}_1^a\neq\boldsymbol{q}_2^a$, we have that $\boldsymbol{y}_{s1}^\nu\neq\boldsymbol{y}_{s2}^\nu$. Therefore, measurements designed based on $\boldsymbol{H}^\nu$ are sufficient for beam discovery.

3.5.2 Resilience to Errors

We are going to show that the encoded syndromes $\boldsymbol{y}_s^\nu$ are more tolerant to the occurrence of measurement errors. Since the mapping functions $\mathcal{D}()$ finds the correct $\boldsymbol{q}^a$ using l^2-norm minimization methods (this is true for both look-up table and search methods), then it is intuitively beneficial to separate the channel syndrome vectors, in the l^2-norm sense, as much as possible. Thus, we want to show that if two channel syndromes $\boldsymbol{y}_{s_1}$ and $\boldsymbol{y}_{s_2}$ (corresponding to channel vectors $\boldsymbol{q}_1^a$ and $\boldsymbol{q}_1^a$) have distance $\delta(\boldsymbol{y}_{s_1}, \boldsymbol{y}_{s_2})$, then their corresponding encoded syndromes are such that

$$\delta(\boldsymbol{y}_{s_1}^\nu, \boldsymbol{y}_{s_2}^\nu) \geq \delta(\boldsymbol{y}_{s_1}, \boldsymbol{y}_{s_2}) \tag{3.5.4}$$

$$\iff \quad \left\| \boldsymbol{y}_{s_1}^\nu - \boldsymbol{y}_{s_2}^\nu \right\| \geq \left\| \boldsymbol{y}_{s_1} - \boldsymbol{y}_{s_2} \right\| \tag{3.5.5}$$

Proposition 3.5.1. *Let $\boldsymbol{G}_c$ be the generator matrix of some LBC code C. Then, if $\boldsymbol{G}_c$ is represented in the standard form and $\boldsymbol{H}^\nu$ is generated using $\boldsymbol{G}_c$ (as $\boldsymbol{G}_c^T \boldsymbol{H}$ (mod 2)), then $\left\| \boldsymbol{y}_{s_1}^\nu - \boldsymbol{y}_{s_2}^\nu \right\| \geq \left\| \boldsymbol{y}_{s_1} - \boldsymbol{y}_{s_2} \right\|$.*

Proposition 3.5.1 shows that by using any appropriate systematic code, we obtain encoded channel syndromes, $\boldsymbol{y}_s^\nu$, that have greater l^2-distance than the original syndromes $\boldsymbol{y}_s$. Hence, we increase the space allowed for the noise-corrupted measurement vector $\boldsymbol{u}_s$ to lie in, while still being able to identify its true corresponding, error-free, channel syndrome. The proof of Proposition 3.5.1 is provided in Appendix A.1.

3.6 Performance Evaluation

3.6.1 Simulation Setup and Parameters

We consider an $n_r \times n_t$ mm-wave channel with noise power per symbol $N_0=-95\text{dBm}$, and average path loss $\mu=136dB$. A maximum number of k (strong) paths exist between TX and RX. A strong path is defined such that its path attenuation is not higher than 14dB above the average path loss, i.e. total path loss is at most 150dB.

Let τ be the time duration of a pilot sequence of one measurement. For simplicity, let $\tau=1$. Also, recall that SNR is defined for a single path (see equation (2.0.7)), and that P is the corresponding transmitted power (i.e., per path). Let the total transmitted power be P_t, where P_t is an integer multiple of P that depends on the number of combined transmit and receive directions (recall Fig. 3.2). Then, the total energy required for beam discovery is $E=mP_t\tau=mP_t$, where m is the total number of measurements[6]. Let the normalized energy be $E_t \triangleq \dfrac{E}{N_0}|\alpha_{\min}/\mu|^2$.

To map the channel measurements to their corresponding angular channels, we use the search method presented in Section 3.4.4. Finally, for every simulation scenario, we obtain the average performance across 10^5 runs.

3.6.2 Performance metrics

To asses the performance of the proposed beam discovery method, we mainly focus on three basic criteria, namely, ***accuracy of beam discovery***, ***number of measurements***, and ***accuracy of path gain value estimates***. To that end, we use the following performance metrics:

i) ***Number of measurements:*** This represents the number of pilots sent from TX to discover the paths to RX.

ii) ***Probability of strongest k beams discovery:*** This denotes the probability of correctly identifying the directions of k_i strong reflectors among k. There are

---

[6]This formula for total energy assumes equal P_t for all measurements. Depending on the employed LBC, this might not always be the case. More generally, we can find the total energy to be: $E = \sum_i m_i P_{t_i}$, where m_i is the number of measurements with total transmit power P_{t_i}.

two cases we consider pertaining to the possibility of the algorithm identifying exactly k_i directions or more than k_i directions at the output: **1) perfect k_i beam discovery:** where exactly k_i true paths are discovered with no incorrect paths among them. **2) all k_i beam discovery:** where k_i true paths are discovered with potentially more incorrectly identified paths.

iii) ***Number of incorrect beams:*** Due to the possibility of obtaining a combination of correct and incorrect paths, it is important that we have as few incorrect beams as possible since further refinement would be made easier.

iv) ***Normalized mean squared error (MSE):*** $\dfrac{\left\| Q^a - \widehat{Q}^a \right\|_F^2}{\left\| Q^a \right\|_F^2}$. Measurement errors occur in the form of 1) imperfect estimates of path gains and phases, and 2) incorrect beam discovery. Hence, MSE provides an conclusive metric for how close the estimated channel matrix is to the true one.

Measurement errors mainly occur due to two contributing factors. The first is ***measurement noise***, and the second is ***quantization*** (recall that we assume the measurements to be quantized using mid-tread ADC quantizers with 2^b+1 levels). In Sections 3.6.3 and 3.6.4, we assess the performance of Beam Discovery approach against ***only*** the effect of measurements noise. We do so by assuming a perfect, infinite resolution ADC. Then, in Section 3.6.5, we investigate the system performance at different ADC resolution levels. This separate investigation of sources of errors allows us to understand how each source affects the performance. Thus, enabling full realization of potential gains of Beam Discovery approach.

3.6.3   Single-path channels

Consider a 15×15 mm-wave channel with $k=1$ path between TX and RX. Hence, the parity check matrix of $(15, 11, 3)$ Hamming code can be used to design both

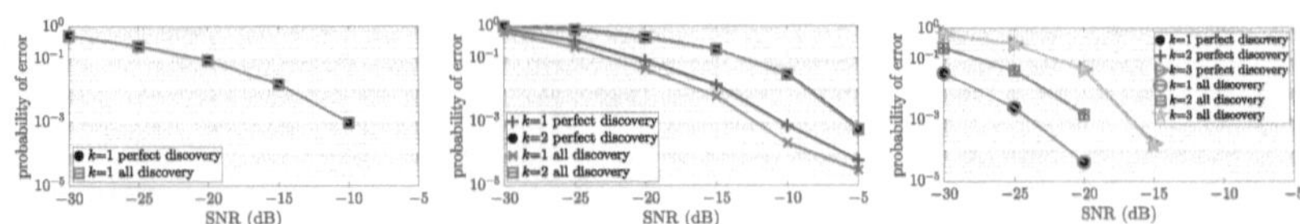

(a) 15×15 channel with k=1. (b) 8×8 channel with k=2. (c) 32×32 channel with k=3.

Figure 3.3: Beam detection probability.

the precoders, f_j, and rx-combiners, w_i, i.e., H_r and H_t, are identical. Hence, we need a number of TX measurements m_r, which is identical to the number of RX measurements m_t=15−11=4. Hence, the total number of measurements is m=16. On the other hand, the exhaustive scanning method requires 225 measurements to inspect every possible TX-RX beam combination. Thus, our approach results in ≈92.8% reduction in the required number of measurements.

We plot the **probability of error** vs. *SNR* for: i) *Perfect* beam discovery where only the single strongest path (k=1) is correctly identified, and ii) *all* beam discovery where the strongest path is correctly identified among potentially other misidentified paths. Fig. 3.3a shows those curves. We observe that both curves are on top of each other which indicates that the strongest path is either correctly detected or is completely missed. Moreover, at all *SNR* values $\geq -$5dB, the probability of error is lower than 10^{-5}, and hence, is not shown here since the shown figures are the averages of 10^5 simulation runs.

In Fig. 3.4, we plot the normalized mean squared error of the channel estimate $\widehat{Q}^a$. The very high values at low signal to noise ratios indicate that $\widehat{Q}^a$ has large components at truly zero components in Q^a and/or large components in Q^a are not represented in $\widehat{Q}^a$. Nevertheless, MSE drops steadily fast as *SNR* increases; indicating improved channel estimation.

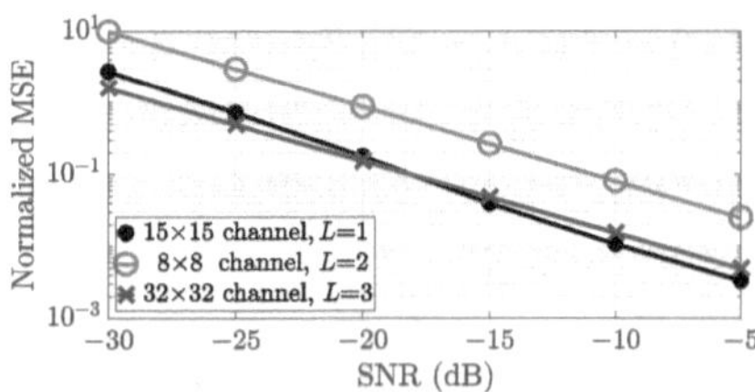

Figure 3.4: Normalized mean squared error (MSE) (assume $L = k$)

When we talk about the possibility of misidentified beams for the all beam discovery metric, it is crucial to have a small number of incorrect beam which would facilitate further refinement. Interestingly, for this scenario, since the error performance of perfect and all beam discovery are the same, we do not have any misidentified paths besides the correct one. Nevertheless, this is not always the case as we will see in further investigated scenarios.

3.6.4   Multi-path Channels

First, consider an 8×8 channel with $k=2$ paths. For this scenario, we use an $(8, 2, 5)$ code for both $\boldsymbol{H_r}$ and $\boldsymbol{H_t}$. With this code, a total number, 36, of measurements is needed for beam discovery. Compared with the 64 measurements needed for exhaustive scanning, we achieve $\approx$43.7% reduction in the number of measurements under this scenario.

Since we investigate a channel that potentially has two strong paths, we evaluate the probability of error of picking one correct strong path ($k=1$) as well as picking two strong paths ($k=2$). Fig. 3.3b depicts the corresponding probability of error of the perfect and all k beam discovery metrics. Unlike single-path channels, there exists a wider gap between perfect and all beam discovery curves for the $k=1$ metric; which indicates higher vulnerability to picking incorrect paths. On the other hand, for k=2, the error performance of the perfect and all beam discovery metrics are almost on top of each other. In Fig. 3.4, similar trend for normalized MSE is obtained where MSE steadily drops as SNR increases.

Recall that in the 15×15 single-path channel investigation, no incorrect paths were obtained alongside correctly identified strong paths. This behavior is not replicated for the 8×8 channel under investigation. For instance, at -10dB we obtain a maximum of 2 misidentified paths. Further, the probability of obtaining incorrect paths at -10dB is ≈ 0.04637.

We further consider a larger array with dimensions 32×32 and k=3 paths. We use a $(32, 16, 8)$ Reed-Muller code to design both $\boldsymbol{H_r}$ and $\boldsymbol{H_t}$. This corresponds to m_r=m_t=16, i.e., total number of measurements m=265. This is 75% fewer measurements needed compared to exhaustive scanning which requires 1024 measurements for beam discovery.

The probability of error for perfect and all k=1, 2, 3 beam discovery are shown in Fig. 3.3c. We notice a faster decay rate for the probability of error. This behavior is due to the higher gain of the TX and RX antenna arrays; which increases the receive signal to noise ratios compared to small arrays. The normalized MSE is shown in 3.4 have similar trend to the previous investigated scenarios.

3.6.5   Effect of Quantization

In this section, both sources of errors are incorporated. Specifically, we analyze the system performance at different ADC resolution levels. We will show that very low resolution ADCs can have detrimental effect on performance. Thus, a natural question that we try to answer in this study is: ***How far should we increase the***

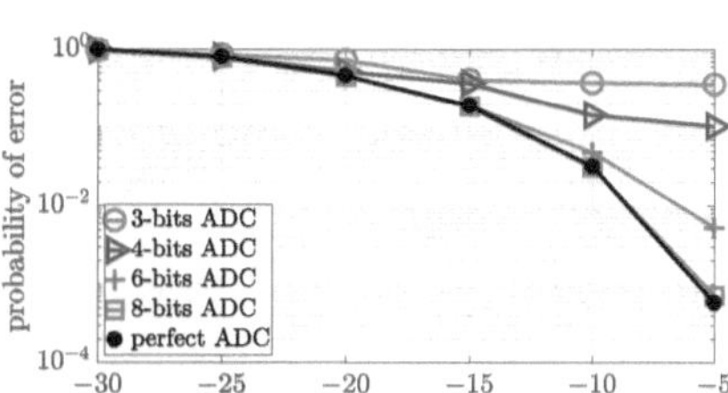

Figure 3.5: Perfect k=2 beam discovery at different quantization resolution (8×8 channel with k=2)

resolution of quantizers in order to unlock the full potential of the Beam Discovery approach?

Recall that we use mid-tread ADCs with 2^b+1 quantization levels (b stands for the number of bits required to represent the ADC output (approximately)). We limit our discussion to the case of 8×8 channels with k=2 paths since its results are representative of the other previously investigated scenarios. For clarity and legibility of figures, we only plot the perfect k=2 beam discovery for $b = 3, 4, 6, 8$ bits i.e., the corresponding number of quanization levels is $9, 17, 65, 257$, respectively. We also plot the corresponding probability of error using a perfect ADC (i.e., $b \to \infty$). These curves are shown in Fig. 3.5.

We find that, at b=3, the probability of error is very high and does not improve with increasing *SNR*. Hence, quantization is the dominant source of errors. Then, as the resolution of ADCs increase, significant performance improvement can be achieved. For instance, while b=4 still do not produce very good probability of error (with increasing *SNR*), a huge leap in performance can be obtained using ADCs with only b=6 bits. Moreover, at b=8, we approach the performance of perfect ADCs. Note that we just need 2 ADCs as per our proposed receiver architecture (see Fig. 2.1).

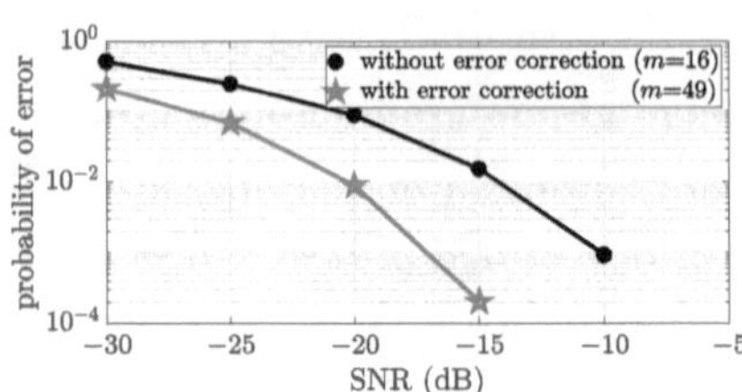

Figure 3.6: Beam detection probability (15×15 channel with k=1)

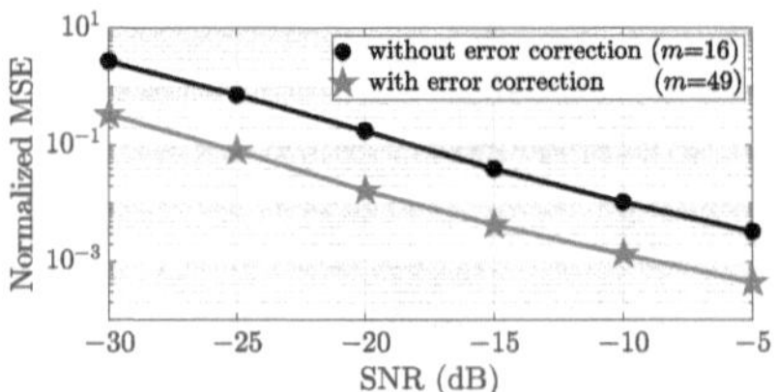

Figure 3.7: MSE (15×15 channel with k=1)

3.6.6 Error Correction

In this section, we investigate the performance of Beam Discovery with the ***error correction*** technique proposed in Section3.5. Recall that error correction is a *channel-coding-like* technique that allows for improving the error performance on the expense of increased number of measurements.

Single-Path Channel

Consider the 15×15 single-path channel we studied in Section 3.6.3. Recall that we used the parity check matrix of $(15, 11, 3)$ Hamming code for both $\boldsymbol{H_r}$ and $\boldsymbol{H_t}$ which resulted in syndromes $\boldsymbol{y_s}$ of length m_r=m_t=4. Now, we need to encode sequences of length 4 into longer sequences $\boldsymbol{y_s^\nu}$ using a systematic code. Conveniently, we can

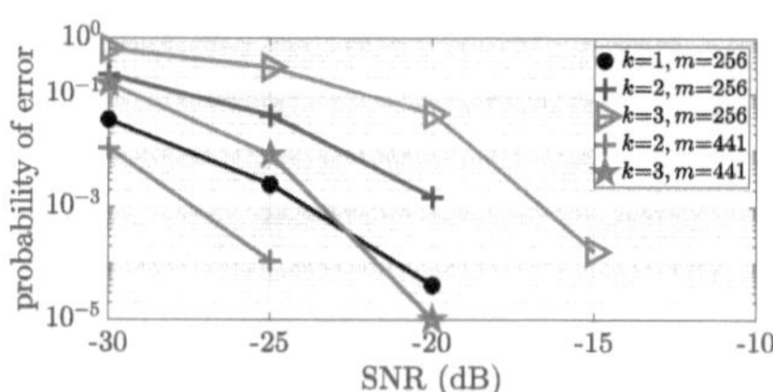

Figure 3.8: Beam detection probability (32×32 channel with k=3)

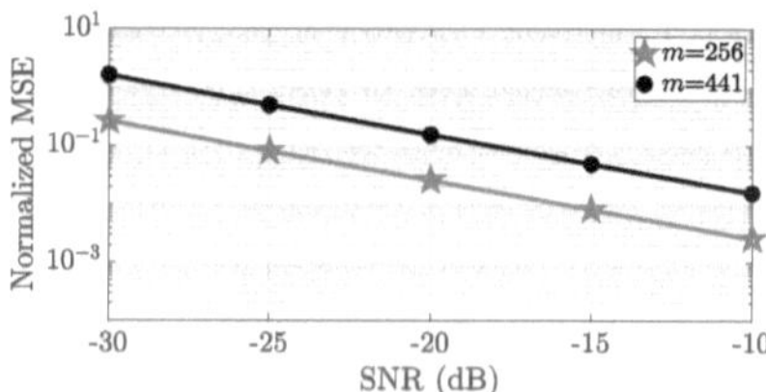

Figure 3.9: MSE (32×32 channel with k=3)

use the $(7, 4, 3)$ Hamming code which maps sequences of length 4 into sequences of length 7. The corresponding $\boldsymbol{H}_r^{\nu}$ and $\boldsymbol{H}_t^{\nu}$ matrices are of size 7×15 and we have that $m_{c_r}=m_{c_t}=7$. Hence we have a total number of measurements for Beam Discovery with error correction $m_c=49$. This is $\approx 78.2\%$ fewer measurements compared to exhaustive scanning. Recall that the number of measurements without error correction is 16.

The probability of error for perfect k=1 beam discovery is depicted in Fig. 3.6. A notable performance improvement over the m=16 case is obtained. That is, at the same SNR, significantly lower probability of error is achieved. This performance improvement is also reflected in the MSE curves in Fig. 3.7.

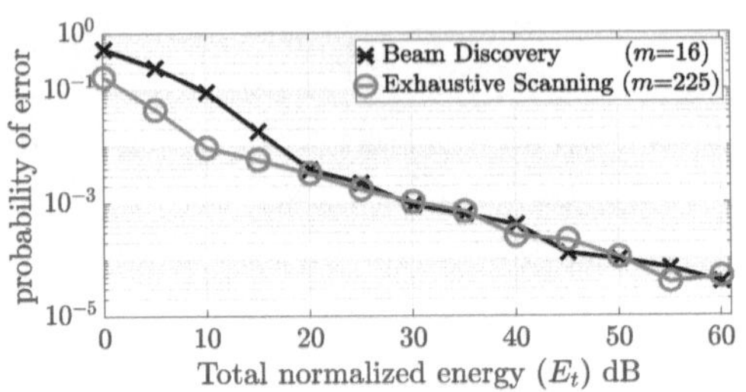

Figure 3.10: Perfect k=1 beam discovery.
Beam Discovery vs. Scanning (15×15 channel with k=1)

Multi-Path Channel

We study 32×32 channels with k= 3 paths. Recall that, in Section3.6.4, we use a $(32, 16, 8)$ Reed-Muller code for which the parity check matrices $\boldsymbol{H_r}$=$\boldsymbol{H_t}$ are of size 16×32. Under this setting we obtain 75% reduction in the number of channel measurements compared to exhaustive scanning (256 instead of 1024 measurements). To add the error correction capability, we encode the channel syndromes using a $(21, 16, 3)$ code (a subcode of the $(31, 26, 3)$ Hamming code). We obtain $\boldsymbol{H_r^{\nu}}$=$\boldsymbol{H_t^{\nu}}$ of size 21×32. Thus, m_{c_r}=m_{c_t}=21 (m_c=441), which gives a reduction of $\approx 57\%$ in number of measurements compared to exhaustive scanning.

For clarity, we only plot the probability of error for perfect k=1, 2, 3 beam discovery shown in Fig. 3.8. Note that at m_c=441, the k=1 perfect beam discovery achieves error probability below 10^{-5}, hence, it is not shown in Fig. 3.8. We notice a huge performance improvement over the m=265 case, that is, at fixed SNR we obtain at least an order of magnitude improvement in the probability of error. We also obtain a corresponding improvement in MSE shown in Fig. 3.9.

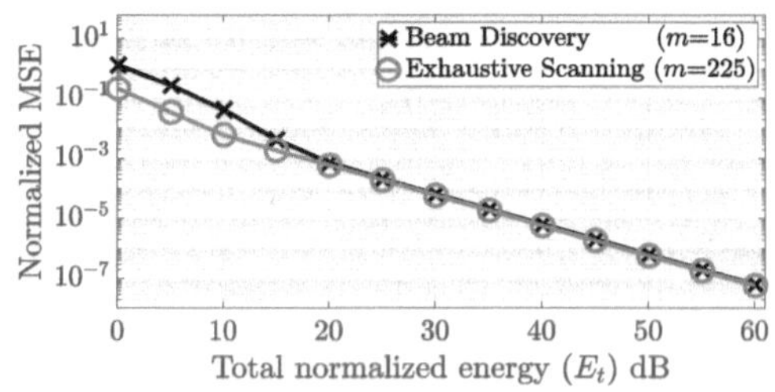

Figure 3.11: Normalized MSE.
Beam Discovery vs. Scanning (15×15 channel with k=1)

3.6.7 Comparison to Exhaustive Scanning

In the previous analysis, we have shown that our devised approach requires significantly fewer measurements for beam discovery when compared to Exhaustive Scanning. Although Scanning entails a large number of measurements, its transmit power P_t is kept low since it only requires pilot transmission over one TX-RX beam combination. On the other hand, our Beam Discovery approach requires transmission over multiple TX-RX beam combinations, which necessitates more invested transmission power in order to keep SNR equal to the one obtained from Scanning. In other words, if we keep P_t fixed for both schemes, then Beam Discovery will operate at lower SNR. This is common in mm-wave channel estimation.

We evaluate the performance of our proposed approach vs. E_t, and compare it against Exhaustive Scanning. Recall that E_t is the total normalized energy required for beam discovery process. To neutralize the effect of quantization, we assume perfect ADCs for both schemes. Due to space limitation, we limit our discussion to only 15×15 single-path channels.

In Fig. 3.10, we plot the probability of error for perfect k=1 beam discovery with m=16, and for exhaustive scanning (m=225). We find that at E_t above 20dB, we achieve almost the same error performance as Scanning, yet, with 92.8% fewer measurements. This is further emphasized by MSE curves shown in Fig. 3.11.

3.7 Conclusion

This chapter provides a solution for the mm-wave channel estimation problem by exploiting its sparse nature in the angular domain. The proposed solution is a beam discovery technique that is similar to error discovery in channel coding. We show that our proposed technique can significantly reduce the number of measurements required for reliable channel estimation. Our solution takes into account the size of TX/RX arrays and the sparsity level of the channel. We determine the number of measurements and the design of each measurement in a deterministic way; based on parity check matrices of appropriately selected LBCs. Under no measurement errors, our solution is guaranteed to find all available beams (paths) between TX and RX. However, due to the presence of channel noise and quantization (ADCs), measurement errors occur, which might cause incorrect beam discovery. Hence, we assess the performance of the proposed scheme under different levels of SNR and ADC resolutions. We further provide a technique for error correction that is also inspired by channel coding. A special case of uncoded discovery within our general coded discovery framework is Exhaustive Scanning. We compare our solution against Scanning and find that we approach its error performance under the same total energy expenditure.

CHAPTER 4

CHANNEL MEASUREMENT BY SOURCE CODING

4.1   Introduction

An interesting question that arises now, having established a framework with analogy to channel coding, is: How small can the number of measurements be for a particular channel structure? In other words, we need to derive the fundamental lower bound on the number of channel measurements required by our proposed solution. The answer to this question is not straightforward given the current perception of the problem, i.e., as a channel coding analogy. Hence, we draw another, more direct analogy to the problem of source coding, which readily allows us to derive the required bound.

Here, sparse MIMO channel estimation is also treated as that of path/beam discovery. We solve this problem using a technique inspired by ***binary source coding (data compression)***. Although binary codes are natively designed to compress binary data, we provide a foundation for the same codes to be used for compressing complex-valued data, as well. We devise a method to obtain channel measurements such that they resemble a compressed version of the channel matrix.

To estimate the channel from the acquired measurements, we train a Deep Neural Network (DNN) that enables very high speed processing. This constitutes an alternative machine learning based measurement decoding method to the look-up table and search methods we propose for the channel-coding-based measurement design.

60

Training DNNs that jointly process all measurements, however, poses an overwhelming complexity. Thus, we propose a novel computationally-tractable solution that sequentially processes the acquired measurements. This method is powerful in the sense that it reduces the problem of estimating the *channel matrix* as a whole into several smaller sub-problems of estimating the individual rows and columns of that matrix. The key contributions of this work are as follows:

- We show that lossless, fixed-rate, linear source codes can be used to design efficient channel measurements that can be *uniquely* mapped to the underlying channels.

- We accurately evaluate the number of measurements needed for reliable channel discovery (as opposed to a mere scaling law). This number is dependent on the compression ratio of the chosen code.

- We present a tight lower bound on the number of measurements needed to reliably discover the channel and provide a solution that achieves this bound.

- We propose a high-performance DNN based measurement-to-channel mapping.

- We show that our solution outperforms the state-of-the-art compressed sensing based solutions and the IEEE 802.11ad beam alignment method.

4.2   Motivating Example

Consider an RX equipped with an antenna array which can form 8 distinct beams. These 8 beams divide the angular space into resolvable directions, i.e., $d_1, d_2, \ldots, d_8$, as shown in Fig. 4.1. The RX needs to establish a Line of Sight (LoS) communication link with TX. This requires some sort of "searching" over the angular space at both TX and RX. For ease of illustration, let us reduce the link establishment problem to

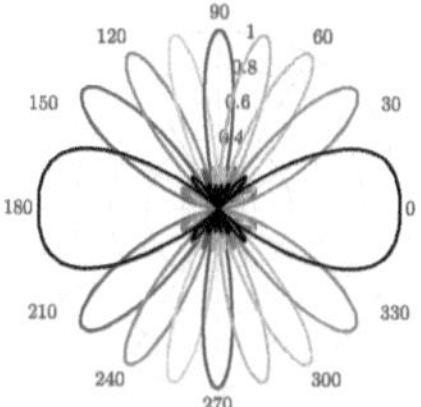

Figure 4.1: Antenna sectors corresponding to angular directions $\{d_i\}_{i=1}^8$.

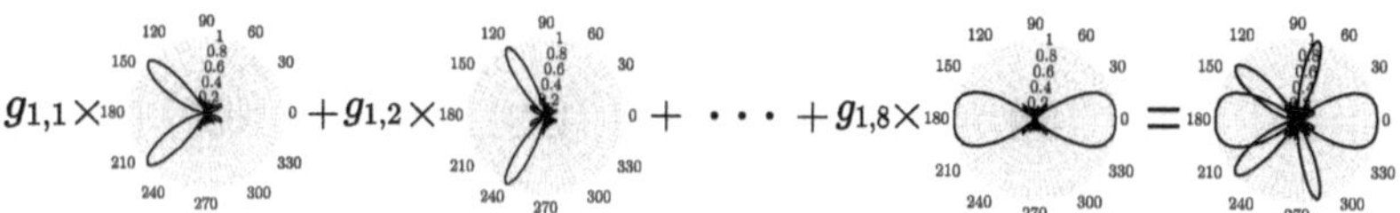

Figure 4.2: Generating the beam pattern required for the 1st measurement (y_1^s)

that of "Angle of Arrival (AoA) discovery" at RX by assuming that TX transmits its signals omnidirectionally. Let the path gain of LoS be denoted by α, which can take arbitrary values. For simplicity of notation, let us assume $\alpha = 1$.

Our ***objective*** is: Find the specific direction d_{i*} which contains the LoS path to TX using the ***least possible number of measurements***. To do so, we envisage the measurement process as ***lossless***, ***fixed-rate channel compression***. This enables *harnessing the power of source compression codes to minimize the number of measurements*. It also enables deriving lower bounds on the number of measurements, using which we can accurately find the LoS (or conclude it is blocked). We propose a measurement approach which has a ***predetermined*** measurement sequence that (1) does not require feedback and (2) is capable of finding the LoS path, no matter in which d_i it exists. Therefore, a constant number of measurements, m, is needed for all d_i.

Angular Channel $\boldsymbol{q}^{a^T}$		Channel measurement $\boldsymbol{y}^{s^T}$
d_0	$[0\,0\,0\,0\,0\,0\,0\,0]$	$[0\,0\,0\,0]$
d_1	$[1\,0\,0\,0\,0\,0\,0\,0]$	$[1\,0\,0\,0]$
d_2	$[0\,1\,0\,0\,0\,0\,0\,0]$	$[0\,1\,0\,0]$
d_3	$[0\,0\,1\,0\,0\,0\,0\,0]$	$[0\,0\,1\,0]$
$\vdots$	$\vdots$	$\vdots$
d_8	$[0\,0\,0\,0\,0\,0\,0\,1]$	$[1\,1\,0\,1]$

Table 4.1: Channel measurements $\boldsymbol{y}^s$ corresponding to all $\boldsymbol{q}^a \in \mathcal{Q}^a$

The key idea of LoS discovery using non-feedback linear source coding is to: 1) Construct a *binary* codebook that represents the angular channel, 2) Find a proper fixed-rate linear source code that losslessly compresses all codewords in that codebook, and 3) Use this code to design the measurements. These steps can be elucidated as follows: **i)** Constructing the codebook is as easy as finding all possible *binary* vectors that represent the LoS position. Since $\alpha=1$, this codebook is exactly the set of all possible channel vectors. Let the channel between TX and RX be denoted by $\boldsymbol{q}^a$, and let $\mathcal{Q}^a$ be the set of all possible channels. The channel $\boldsymbol{q}^a \in \mathcal{Q}^a$ has 8 components; each one represents the path gain corresponding to a unique angular sector as shown in Fig. 4.1. Table 4.1 shows all possible $\boldsymbol{q}^a$ in our setup (for arbitrary gain values, simply replace the '1's in Table 4.1 with α). **ii)** Choose the linear source code, denoted by its generator matrix $\boldsymbol{G}$ as:

$$\boldsymbol{G} = \begin{pmatrix} 1 & 0 & 0 & 0 & 1 & 0 & 0 & 1 \\ 0 & 1 & 0 & 0 & 1 & 1 & 0 & 1 \\ 0 & 0 & 1 & 0 & 0 & 1 & 1 & 0 \\ 0 & 0 & 0 & 1 & 0 & 0 & 1 & 1 \end{pmatrix} \tag{4.2.1}$$

To compress $\boldsymbol{q}^a$, we simply need to find the matrix multiplication $\boldsymbol{y}^s = \boldsymbol{G}\boldsymbol{q}^a$ (see Table 4.1). **iii)** Design the measurements such that $\boldsymbol{y}^s$ is imitated by the measurement results. ***This is done by beamforming at RX***. Notice that the ith measurement, i.e., y_i^s (the ith component of $\boldsymbol{y}^s$) is the multiplication of the ith row of $\boldsymbol{G}$ by $\boldsymbol{q}^a$. Mathematically, this is just adding all elements q_j^a of $\boldsymbol{q}^a$ which corresponds to $g_{i,j}=1$, ($g_{i,j}$ is the element at row i, and column j in $\boldsymbol{G}$). That is

$$y_i^s = \sum_{j=1}^{8} q_j^a \times g_{i,j} = \sum_{j:\, g_{i,j}=1} q_j^a. \tag{4.2.2}$$

Hence, measurement i should only contain the directions d_j whose corresponding $g_{i,j}$ equals 1, and exclude the rest (Notice that we can map the ith row of $\boldsymbol{G}$ to the ith measurement and the jth column to the jth sector (direction d_j)). Essentially, this means that in each of the measurements y_i^s, we combine the signals received at a specific set of AoA directions This can be realized by carefully shaping the antenna pattern using beamforming. Fig. 4.2 highlights this process for the 1st measurement in which only the direction d_1, d_5 and d_8 are included. *The measurement results $\forall d_i$ are shown in Table 4.1.* Note that the number of required measurements is 4 for all d_i.

Lower Bound: A fundamental question that arises here is: *Can we find a better fixed-rate, lossless source code (other than the one given in Eq. (4.2.1)) that would produce fewer measurements, and hence increase the efficiency of the measurement process?* To answer this question, we need to find **the minimum expected number of measurements** required to discover the channel using our proposed source coding solution. This number is identical to the minimum average code length (over all fixed-rate, lossless codes). The minimum average code length is well-known to be lower bounded by the ***Shannon Entropy***; denoted by H_2 and defined as

$$H_2\left(\boldsymbol{q}^a\right) = \sum_{q^a \in \mathcal{Q}^a} \mathbb{P}\left(\boldsymbol{q}^a\right) \log_2\left(\frac{1}{\mathbb{P}\left(\boldsymbol{q}^a\right)}\right) \tag{4.2.3}$$

Calculating $H_2(\boldsymbol{q^a})$ requires knowledge of the probability distribution $\mathbb{P}(\boldsymbol{q^a})$. Fixed-rate codes, however, do not account for the frequency of $\boldsymbol{q^a}$ (hence, the mapping to equal-length codes). By limiting the space of codes to be over fixed-rate codes, we can improve the bound to be

$$\lceil \log_2(|\mathcal{Q}^a|) \rceil \geq H_2(\boldsymbol{q^a}) \tag{4.2.4}$$

where $|\mathcal{Q}^a| = 9$ (recall that there exists 9 possible scenarios for $\boldsymbol{q^a}$ as shown in Table 4.1). This tighter bound is obtained by assuming a *Uniform* distribution, which is the entropy maximizing distribution, over the channel space $\mathcal{Q}^a$. Eq. (4.2.4) reveals that our chosen code achieves the lower bound of 4 measurements. We provide a formal discussion on the lower bound in Section 4.4.4.

Remark 4.2.0.1. *This Motivating Example only dealt with a simplified channel model, with only one channel path and a fixed path gain of $\alpha = 1$. However, in the rest of the chapter, we will consider generalized channel models with possibly several paths of arbitrary path gain values, i.e., $\alpha \in \mathbb{C}$.*

4.3 Problem Formulation

The problem we need to solve is to minimize the number of measurements $m = m_t \times m_r$ such that $\boldsymbol{Q}$ can be reliably reconstructed. This problem can be mathematically stated as:

$$
\begin{aligned}
P1: \underset{\boldsymbol{w}_i, \boldsymbol{f}_j, \mathcal{D}}{\text{minimize}} \quad & m_t \times m_r \\
\text{subject to} \quad & y^s_{i,j} = \boldsymbol{w}_i^H \boldsymbol{Q} \boldsymbol{f}_j, \\
& \mathcal{D}(\{y^s_{i,j}\}) = \boldsymbol{Q}^a.
\end{aligned}
\tag{4.3.1}
$$

Note that $y_{i,j}^s$ exists $\forall i, j \in \{1, \ldots, m_r\} \times \{1, \ldots, m_t\}$. That is, measurements are taken using all combinations of $\boldsymbol{f}_j$ and $\boldsymbol{w}_i$. We also use $s = 1$. The design variables are the tx-precoders $\boldsymbol{f}_j$, the rx-combiners $\boldsymbol{w}_i$ and the decoding function $\mathcal{D}$. We do not explicitly consider the impact of errors in this formulation but its effect will be studied in Section 4.4.5. Note also that due to the use of VGAs at each antenna element, the constant modulus constraint on $\boldsymbol{f}_j$ and $\boldsymbol{w}_i$, that is often incorporated in analog beamforming designs, is not needed.

4.4 Source-Coding-Based Measurements

In this section, we formally introduce *mm-wave beam discovery* as a source coding problem. We initially focus on channels with single-transmit, multiple-receive antennas. Specifically, we provide the conditions under which a chosen fixed-rate source code can be used to uniquely *"encode"* channel vectors in $\mathbb{C}^{n_r}$ into measurement vectors of fewer components. This setting is **identical to that of multiple-transmit, single-receive antennas.** In Section 4.5, we show how to use DNNs to *"decode"* the measurements and obtain an estimate for the observed channel. Then, in Section 4.6, we consider general channels with multiple TX and RX antennas. Now, let us start with the following discussion on source codes.

4.4.1 Source Codes

Let C be a binary *linear* source code with encoding and decoding functions denoted by $\mathcal{E}_{\mathbb{F}_2}$ and $\mathcal{D}_{\mathbb{F}_2}$, respectively. We refer to C as the encoding-decoding function pair $(\mathcal{E}_{\mathbb{F}_2}, \mathcal{D}_{\mathbb{F}_2})$. The subscript $\mathbb{F}_2$ denotes the finite field of two elements $0_{\mathbb{F}_2}$ and $1_{\mathbb{F}_2}$ (also referred to as $GF(2)$) over which the code C is defined. Later on, we will drop the subscripts to simplify notation as long as they can be inferred from the context.

Definition 4.4.1 (Linear Source Code). *A source code C whose encoding function $\mathcal{E}_{\mathbb{F}_2}$ is a linear function of the source sequences is called a **linear source code**.*

Let $\boldsymbol{s}$ be a source sequence of length n where $\boldsymbol{s} \in \mathcal{S} \subseteq \{0_{\mathbb{F}_2}, 1_{\mathbb{F}_2}\}^n$, and let $\boldsymbol{c_s} \in \mathcal{I}_\mathcal{S} \subseteq \{0_{\mathbb{F}_2}, 1_{\mathbb{F}_2}\}^m$ be its associated binary representation under C where $\mathcal{I}_\mathcal{S}$ is the image of $\mathcal{S}$ under $\mathcal{E}_{\mathbb{F}_2}$. Thus, using a linear source code C, we can find the representation of $\boldsymbol{s}$ under C using

$$\boldsymbol{c_s} = \boldsymbol{G}\boldsymbol{s}, \tag{4.4.1}$$

where $\boldsymbol{G} \in \{0_{\mathbb{F}_2}, 1_{\mathbb{F}_2}\}^{m \times n}$ is called the **generator matrix**. Note that linearity guarantees fixed-rate since the code length is a constant value (equals the number of rows of $\boldsymbol{G}$).

The decoding function $\mathcal{D}_{\mathbb{F}_2}$, maps sequences $\boldsymbol{c_s}$ to a corresponding source sequence $\hat{\boldsymbol{s}} \in \hat{\mathcal{S}} \subseteq \{0_{\mathbb{F}_2}, 1_{\mathbb{F}_2}\}^n$. Suppose that $\mathcal{S}$ is the set of all sequences such that if $\boldsymbol{s}_1, \boldsymbol{s}_2 \in \mathcal{S}$, we have that $\boldsymbol{s}_1 \neq \boldsymbol{s}_2 \overset{\text{iff}}{\Longleftrightarrow} \boldsymbol{c}_{\boldsymbol{s}1} \neq \boldsymbol{c}_{\boldsymbol{s}2}$. In other words, $\mathcal{E}_{\mathbb{F}_2} : \mathcal{S} \to \mathcal{I}_\mathcal{S}$ is injective (one-to-one). Consequently, if we define the function $\mathcal{D}_{\mathbb{F}_2}$ over $\mathcal{I}_\mathcal{S}$ as the inverse function of $\mathcal{E}_{\mathbb{F}_2}$, i.e., $\mathcal{E}_{\mathbb{F}_2}^{-1} \triangleq \mathcal{D}_{\mathbb{F}_2} : \mathcal{I}_\mathcal{S} \to \mathcal{S}$, then we have that $\hat{\boldsymbol{s}} = \mathcal{D}_{\mathbb{F}_2}\left(\mathcal{E}_{\mathbb{F}_2}\left(\boldsymbol{s}\right)\right) = \boldsymbol{s}, \ \forall \boldsymbol{s} \in \mathcal{S}$.

4.4.2 MmWave Beam Discovery

Let $\boldsymbol{q}^a \in \mathbb{C}^{n_r}$ denote the angular **channel vector** between TX and RX. Define $\boldsymbol{q}_s^a \in \{0, 1\}^{n_r}$ to be the **support vector** associated with $\boldsymbol{q}^a$ such that $\boldsymbol{q}_s^a = \begin{pmatrix} q_{s_1}^a & q_{s_2}^a & \cdots & q_{s_{n_r}}^a \end{pmatrix}^T$ where $q_{s_i}^a = 1$ if $q_i^a \neq 0$ and $q_{s_i}^a = 0$ otherwise. More generally, a support vector can be defined as:

Definition 4.4.2 (Support vector). *The support vector $\boldsymbol{v_s}$ associated with an arbitrary $n-$dimensional vector $\boldsymbol{v} \in \mathbb{C}^n$ is a binary vector of the same size that identifies* the non-zero components of $\boldsymbol{v}$ and whose components, v_{si}, are defined as $v_{si} = 1$ if $v_i \neq 0$ and $v_{si} = 0$ if $v_i = 0$.

We further define the set of non-zero indexes $\mathcal{X}_v$ of an arbitrary vector $\boldsymbol{v}$ as follows:

Definition 4.4.3 (Set of Non-Zero Indexes $\mathcal{X}_v$). *For any arbitrary $n-$dimensional vector $\boldsymbol{v}$, we define $\mathcal{X}_v$ as the set of indexes of its non-zero components, i.e., $\mathcal{X}_v = \{i|v_i \neq 0 \,, 0 \leq i \leq n-1\}$.*

Hence, if $\boldsymbol{v}_s$ is the support vector corresponding to $\boldsymbol{v}$, then we have that $\mathcal{X}_v = \mathcal{X}_{v_s}$, since $v_i = 0 \Longleftrightarrow v_{s_i} = 0$. Now, let $\mathcal{Q}^a$ be the set containing all possible channel vectors $\boldsymbol{q}^a$. Also let $\mathcal{Q}_s^a$ be the set of all support vectors $\boldsymbol{q}_s^a$ such that their corresponding channels $\boldsymbol{q}^a \in \mathcal{Q}^a$. An interesting behavior we have for these sets is as follows: If we have a channel $\boldsymbol{q}_1^a$ whose support vector $\boldsymbol{q}_{s_1}^a \in \mathcal{Q}_s^a$, then removing any non-zero component(s) from $\boldsymbol{q}_1^a$ (due to blockage for example) would still yield a valid channel $\boldsymbol{q}_2^a \in \mathcal{Q}^a$, whose support vectors $\boldsymbol{q}_{s_2}^a$ also belongs to $\mathcal{Q}_s^a$. We call this the ***inclusion property***.

Definition 4.4.4. *[Inclusion Properties of $\mathcal{Q}_s^a$]*

(i) *Let $\boldsymbol{q}_{s_1}^a, \boldsymbol{q}_{s_2}^a \in \{0,1\}^{n_r}$ such that $\mathcal{X}_{\boldsymbol{q}_{s_2}^a} \subseteq \mathcal{X}_{\boldsymbol{q}_{s_1}^a}$. If $\boldsymbol{q}_{s_1}^a \in \mathcal{Q}_s^a$, then $\boldsymbol{q}_{s_2}^a \in \mathcal{Q}_s^a$.*

(ii) *$\boldsymbol{0} \in \mathcal{Q}_s^a$. In fact, this is a consequence of property (i) above since for any $\boldsymbol{q}_s^a \in \mathcal{Q}_s^a$, we have that $\mathcal{X}_0 = \varnothing \subseteq \mathcal{X}_{\boldsymbol{q}_s^a}$.*

Now, we are ready to present the theorem that establishes the conditions that need to be satisfied by a linear source code so that each possible channel $\boldsymbol{q}^a$ would result in a ***unique*** measurement vector $\boldsymbol{y}^s$. Impairments under noise are not addressed in this theorem.

Theorem 4.4.1. *Consider a **binary** linear source code C whose encoding function $\mathcal{E}$ (defined by the binary generator matrix $\boldsymbol{G}$) is an injective function defined over $\mathcal{Q}_s^a \in$*

$\{0,1\}^{n_r}$. *If we consider $\boldsymbol{G}$ to be defined over the complex field, then for all channel vectors $\boldsymbol{q}_1^a, \boldsymbol{q}_2^a \in \mathcal{Q}^a \subseteq \mathbb{C}^{n_r}$ we have $\boldsymbol{q}_1^a \neq \boldsymbol{q}_2^a$ if and only if $\boldsymbol{G}\boldsymbol{q}_1^a = \boldsymbol{y}_1^s \neq \boldsymbol{y}_2^s = \boldsymbol{G}\boldsymbol{q}_2^a$.*

Proof. Let $\boldsymbol{q}_1^a, \boldsymbol{q}_2^a \in \mathcal{Q}^a$, and let $\boldsymbol{y}_i^s = \boldsymbol{G}\boldsymbol{q}_i^a$. Now, assume that $\boldsymbol{q}_1^a \neq \boldsymbol{q}_2^a$. Then, we have that

$$\boldsymbol{y}_1^s - \boldsymbol{y}_2^s = \boldsymbol{G}\boldsymbol{q}_1^a - \boldsymbol{G}\boldsymbol{q}_2^a = \boldsymbol{G}\underbrace{(\boldsymbol{q}_1^a - \boldsymbol{q}_2^a)}_{=\boldsymbol{v}} = \boldsymbol{G}\boldsymbol{v} = \sum_{i=1}^{n_r} v_i \times \boldsymbol{g}_i = \sum_{i\in\mathcal{X}_v} v_i \times \boldsymbol{g}_i \quad (4.4.2)$$

where $\boldsymbol{g}_i$ is the ith column of $\boldsymbol{G}$. **To show that $\boldsymbol{y}_1^s - \boldsymbol{y}_2^s \neq 0$, we need to show that all vectors $\boldsymbol{g}_i \; \forall i \in \mathcal{X}_v$, are linearly independent.** Otherwise, if such vectors $\boldsymbol{g}_i$ are linearly **dependent**, then $\exists v_i \in \mathbb{R}$ for $i \in \mathcal{X}_v$ such that $\boldsymbol{y}_1^s - \boldsymbol{y}_2^s = \boldsymbol{G}\boldsymbol{v} = \boldsymbol{0}$.

In fact, we can show a stronger statement: "all vectors $\boldsymbol{g}_i \; \forall i \in \mathcal{X}_{\boldsymbol{q}_1^a} \cup \mathcal{X}_{\boldsymbol{q}_2^a} \supseteq \mathcal{X}_v$, are linearly independent". Note that $\mathcal{X}_{\boldsymbol{q}_1^a}$ and $\mathcal{X}_{\boldsymbol{q}_2^a}$ are the sets of indexes of the non-zero components of $\boldsymbol{q}_1^a$ and $\boldsymbol{q}_2^a$, respectively (recall Definition 4.4.3) and that $\mathcal{X}_{\boldsymbol{q}_1^a} = \mathcal{X}_{\boldsymbol{q}_{s1}^a}$ and $\mathcal{X}_{\boldsymbol{q}_2^a} = \mathcal{X}_{\boldsymbol{q}_{s2}^a}$.

- First, let us show that $\mathcal{X}_v$ is a subset of $\mathcal{X}_{\boldsymbol{q}_1^a} \cup \mathcal{X}_{\boldsymbol{q}_2^a}$.

  Since $v_i = q_{1,i}^a - q_{2,i}^a \; \forall \, 1 \leq i \leq n_r$, then $q_{i,1}^a = q_{i,2}^a = 0 \implies v_i = 0$. Therefore, we have

  $$\mathcal{X}_{\boldsymbol{q}_1^a}^c \cap \mathcal{X}_{\boldsymbol{q}_2^a}^c = \left\{\mathcal{X}_{\boldsymbol{q}_1^a} \cup \mathcal{X}_{\boldsymbol{q}_2^a}\right\}^c \subseteq \mathcal{X}_v^c \qquad (4.4.3)$$

  Then, by taking the complements of both sides we obtain the required result (note that $\{\cdot\}^c$ denotes a set complement).

- Second, we show that vectors in the set $\mathcal{G} \triangleq \{\boldsymbol{g}_i | i \in \mathcal{X}_{\boldsymbol{q}_1^a} \cup \mathcal{X}_{\boldsymbol{q}_2^a}\}$ are linearly independent over $\mathbb{F}_2$: Assume towards contradiction that $\mathcal{G}$ is linearly dependent over $\mathbb{F}_2$. Hence, there exists a set $\mathcal{G}_D \subseteq \mathcal{G}$ such that any $\boldsymbol{g}_{i_0} \in \mathcal{G}_D$ can be written as a linear combination of all other vectors in $\mathcal{G}_D$, i.e.,

$$\boldsymbol{g}_{i_0} = \sum_{\substack{j:j\neq i_0 \\ \boldsymbol{g}_j \in \mathcal{G}_D}} \boldsymbol{g}_j \mod 2. \tag{4.4.4}$$

Note that over $\mathbb{F}_2$, we can assume, without loss of generality (W.L.O.G.), that the coefficients of the linear combination above are 1's. Hence, we have that

$$\sum_{j:\boldsymbol{g}_j \in \mathcal{G}_D} \boldsymbol{g}_j \mod 2 = 0 \tag{4.4.5}$$

Next, assume that $\exists \boldsymbol{q}^a_{s_3}, \boldsymbol{q}^a_{s_4} \in \mathcal{Q}^a_s$ such that $\mathcal{X}_{v_s} = \{j \mid \boldsymbol{g}_j \in \mathcal{G}_D\}$ where $\boldsymbol{v}_s = \boldsymbol{q}^a_{s_3} - \boldsymbol{q}^a_{s_4}$ mod 2.

Then, since $\boldsymbol{G}$ is injective over $\mathcal{Q}^a_s$, then we have that

$$\boldsymbol{G}\boldsymbol{v}_s \mod 2 = \sum_{j \in \mathcal{X}_{v_s}} \boldsymbol{g}_j \mod 2 \tag{4.4.6}$$

$$= \sum_{j:\boldsymbol{g}_j \in \mathcal{G}_D} \boldsymbol{g}_j \mod 2 \neq 0 \xLeftrightarrow{\text{iff}} \boldsymbol{v}_s \mod 2 \neq 0 \tag{4.4.7}$$

But, if $\mathcal{G}_D$ is non-empty, then $\boldsymbol{v}_s \neq 0$. Hence, we arrive at a contradiction to Eq. (4.4.4). Therefore, the set $\mathcal{G}$ is linearly independent over $GF(2)$.

It remains to show that such $\boldsymbol{q}^a_{s_3}$ and $\boldsymbol{q}^a_{s_4}$ indeed exist. Let us construct $\boldsymbol{q}^a_{s_3}$ as follows: First, let $\boldsymbol{q}^a_{s_3} = \boldsymbol{q}^a_{s_1}$, then, reset its ith component to 0 ($q^a_{s_3,i} = 0$) if $\boldsymbol{g}_i \notin \mathcal{G}_D$. Similarly, set $\boldsymbol{q}^a_{s_4} = \boldsymbol{q}^a_{s_2}$, then, reset the ith component to 0 ($q^a_{s_4,i} = 0$) if $\boldsymbol{g}_i \notin \mathcal{G}_D$ OR if $q^a_{s_1,i} = 1$.

Then, by construction, we have $\mathcal{X}_{\boldsymbol{q}^a_{s_3}} \subseteq \mathcal{X}_{\boldsymbol{q}^a_{s_1}}$ and $\mathcal{X}_{\boldsymbol{q}^a_{s_4}} \subseteq \mathcal{X}_{\boldsymbol{q}^a_{s_2}}$. Hence, by the inclusion property (recall Definition 4.4.4) we have $\boldsymbol{q}_{s_3}^a, \boldsymbol{q}_{s_4}^a \in \mathcal{Q}_s^a$ since both $\boldsymbol{q}_{s_1}^a, \boldsymbol{q}_{s_2}^a \in \mathcal{Q}_s^a$. Also, it is easy to see that $q_{s_3,j}^a - q_{s_4,j}^a \mod 2 = 1 \ \forall j : \boldsymbol{g}_j \in \mathcal{G}_D$.

- Third, by Lemma 4.4.1 below, the set $\mathcal{G}$, now taken over $\mathbb{R}$, is linearly independent.

Therefore, in Eq. (4.4.2), it follows that $\boldsymbol{y}_1^s - \boldsymbol{y}_2^s \neq \boldsymbol{0}$ *if and only if* $\boldsymbol{q}_1^a - \boldsymbol{q}_2^a \neq 0$, which concludes the proof. $\qquad\square$

Lemma 4.4.1. *Any set of $n-$dimensional linearly independent vectors over $\mathbb{F}_2$ are also linearly independent over $\mathbb{C}$ if we interpret their $0_{\mathbb{F}_2}$ and $1_{\mathbb{F}_2}$ components to be real scalars.*

The proof is provided in Appendix B.1.

4.4.3   Beamforming Design

Now, we focus our attention on the design of beamforming vectors $\boldsymbol{w}_i$, such that the measurement vector $\boldsymbol{y}^s$ is such that $\boldsymbol{y}^s = \boldsymbol{G}\boldsymbol{q}^a$. Obviously, $\boldsymbol{w}_i$ depends on the chosen source code. Specifically, we want $\boldsymbol{w}_i$ to satisfy

$$\boldsymbol{w}_i^H \boldsymbol{q} = \boldsymbol{y}_i^s = \boldsymbol{g}_i \boldsymbol{q}^a = \sum_{j=1}^{n_r} g_{i,j} q_j^a \tag{4.4.8}$$

where $\boldsymbol{g}_i$ is the ith row of $\boldsymbol{G}$, and $g_{i,j}$ is the jth element of $\boldsymbol{g}_i$. Recall that if n_r antennas exist at RX, then there exists n_r resolvable angular directions. Let us call these directions $d_1, d_2, \ldots d_{n_r}$. We want $\boldsymbol{w}_i$ to combine the received signal components at specific angular directions. Those angular directions are determined by $\boldsymbol{g}_i = \left(g_{i,1}, g_{i,2}, \ldots, g_{i,n_r} \right)$. Specifically, we want $\boldsymbol{w}_i$ to include the signal at directions d_j for all j such that $g_{i,j} = 1$.

Recall that $\boldsymbol{q} = \boldsymbol{U}_r \boldsymbol{q}^a$. Hence, we can rewrite Eq. (4.4.8) as $\boldsymbol{w}_i^H \boldsymbol{q} = \boldsymbol{w}_i^H \boldsymbol{U}_r \boldsymbol{q}^a = \boldsymbol{g}_i \boldsymbol{q}^a$. Thus, we need to design $\boldsymbol{w}_i$ such that $\boldsymbol{w}_i^H \boldsymbol{U}_r = \boldsymbol{g}_i$, which can be rewritten as:

$$\boldsymbol{w}_i^H \left(\boldsymbol{e}_r\left(0\right) \quad \boldsymbol{e}_r\left(\frac{1}{L_r}\right) \quad \cdots \quad \boldsymbol{e}_r\left(\frac{n_r - 1}{L_r}\right) \right) = \boldsymbol{g}_i. \tag{4.4.9}$$

Since the columns of $\boldsymbol{U}_r$ constitute an orthonormal basis, a very simple design of $\boldsymbol{w}_i$ is as a summation of the columns $\boldsymbol{e}_r\left(\frac{j-1}{L_r}\right)$ such that $g_{i,j} = 1$. In other words, we can design $\boldsymbol{w}_i$ as:

$$\boldsymbol{w}_i = \sum_{j:g_{i,j}=1} \boldsymbol{e}_r\left(\frac{j-1}{L_r}\right) \tag{4.4.10}$$

Remark 4.4.1.1. *The adopted beamforming design is ideal under the perfect sparsity assumption (which we adopt). That is when channel paths lie at the angular directions defined in $\boldsymbol{U}_r$. In practice, however, channel paths arrive at arbitrary angles in $[0, 2\pi]$. This makes each path contribute to multiple components in $\boldsymbol{q}^a$, hence, $\boldsymbol{q}^a$ is not perfectly sparse. This happens due to (i) antenna side-lobes, and (ii) beam-overlap. To resolve this problem, we can use side-lobe suppression techniques, e.g. Taylor Window, as well as large antenna arrays, which can form pencil-beam antenna patterns that avoid the beam-overlap problem. These come at the expense of a slight reduction in beam resolution. We leave this investigation for a future study and only focus on the main idea of using source-coding-based measurements.*

4.4.4 On the lower bound on the number of measurements

In Theorem 4.4.1, we showed that a linear source code C which can **uniquely** encode all $\boldsymbol{q}_s^a \in \mathcal{Q}_s^a$ can be used to design a framework that uniquely measures all $\boldsymbol{q}^a \in \mathcal{Q}^a$. Let the compression ratio of the code C be denoted by r_c such that $r_c = \dfrac{m}{n_r}$. where m and n_r are the number of rows and columns of C's generator matrix $\boldsymbol{G}$, respectively.

Reducing the number of measurements is a fundamental objective for the mm-wave beam discovery problem. In light of Theorem 4.4.1, we can see that finding a source code with a high compression rate (small r_c) is crucial for attaining such an objective. In the following discussion, we try to better understand the nature of this lower bound in the context of our proposed solution.

Corollary 4.4.1.1. *Let $\underline{m}$ denote the lowest possible number of measurements for mm-wave beam discovery using lossless, fixed-rate source coding. Then, we have*

$$\underline{m} \geq \left\lceil \log_2 \left(\sum_{i=0}^{k} \binom{n_r}{i} \right) \right\rceil \geq H_2 \left(\boldsymbol{q}_s^a \right) \tag{4.4.11}$$

where $H_2 \left(\cdot \right)$ is the binary entropy function.

Proof. Suppose that C is a linear lossless fixed-rate source code which can uniquely compress all $\boldsymbol{q}_s^a \in \mathcal{Q}_s^a$. By Theorem 4.4.1, we have that the number of measurements needed for estimating the mm-wave channel is equal to m (the length of encoded channel support vectors). Since the length of compressed sequences for any such code is lower bounded by $H_2 \left(\boldsymbol{q}_s^a \right)$, then we have $\underline{m} \geq H_2 \left(\boldsymbol{q}_s^a \right)$. Moreover, since fixed-rate source codes do not take the probability distribution (i.e., frequency) of $\boldsymbol{q}_s^a$ into account, then we have $\underline{m} \geq \sup_{\mathbb{P}(\boldsymbol{q}_s^a)} H_2 \left(\boldsymbol{q}_s^a \right) \geq H_2 \left(\boldsymbol{q}_s^a \right)$, where

$$\sup_{\mathbb{P}(\boldsymbol{q}_s^a)} \sum_{q^a \in \mathcal{Q}^a} \mathbb{P} \left(\boldsymbol{q}_s^a \right) \log_2 \left(\frac{1}{\mathbb{P} \left(\boldsymbol{q}_s^a \right)} \right) = \log_2 \left(|\mathcal{Q}_s^a| \right) \tag{4.4.12}$$

The result of solving the sup problem in Eq. (4.4.12) is $\mathbb{P} \left(\boldsymbol{q}_s^a \right) = \frac{1}{|\mathcal{Q}_s^a|} \; \forall \boldsymbol{q}_s^a$ since the uniform distribution maximizes the entropy. Since the number of measurement has to be an integer, we take the ceil of right hand side of Eq. (4.4.12). Finally, by the inclusion property in Definition 4.4.4, we have $|\mathcal{Q}_s^a| = \sum_{i=0}^{k} \binom{n_r}{i}$, which concludes the proof. $\square$

4.4.5 Channel Estimation Error

In Theorem 4.4.1, we have shown how to obtain unique measurements $\boldsymbol{y}^s \ \forall \ \boldsymbol{q}^a \in \mathcal{Q}^a$. Recall that $\boldsymbol{y}^s = \boldsymbol{G}\boldsymbol{q}^a$ is an error-free measurement vector. In practice, however, measurements are never error-free. Measurements errors are bound to happen due to the effects of **thermal and quantization noise**, among others factors. The quality of channel estimates obtained using error-corrupted measurements is essentially degraded, which calls for a deeper understanding of the effects of such errors. A crucial question we try to answer here is: ***Do small perturbations/imperfections in channel measurements make channel estimates considerably deviate from their true values?*** In this section, we shed some light on this problem by deriving an upper bound on channel estimation error as a function of measurement error. We also show that for a special class of generator matrices, the channel estimation error, measured using the l_2-norm, is smaller than or equal to the l_2 norm of the measurement error.

We denote error-corrupted measurements using $\boldsymbol{u}^s$ such that $\boldsymbol{u}^s = \boldsymbol{y}^s + \boldsymbol{z}$, where $\boldsymbol{z}$ is the measurement error (recall Eq. (2.0.12) and the discussion that follows). Assume that we can **perfectly** decode any measurement vector into its corresponding channel. That is, for any measurement vector $\boldsymbol{y}^s$, we can find a corresponding $\boldsymbol{q}^a$ such that $\boldsymbol{y}^s = \boldsymbol{G}\boldsymbol{q}^a$ (measurement decoding will be further discussed in Section 4.5). Let us also denote the *channel estimate* obtained using error-corrupted measurements $\boldsymbol{u}^s$ by $\hat{\boldsymbol{q}}^a$, i.e., $\boldsymbol{u}^s = \boldsymbol{G}\hat{\boldsymbol{q}}^a$. The following proposition provides an upper bound on the channel estimation error in terms of measurements errors.

Proposition 4.4.1. *Assume perfect measurement decoding, and let $\sigma_{min}\left(\cdot\right)$ denote the minimum singular value of a given matrix. Then, the channel estimation error is* *upper bounded as:*

$$\|\hat{q}^a - q^a\|_2 \leq \frac{1}{\sigma_{min}(G)} \|z\|_2 \qquad (4.4.13)$$

Proof. Let us start by writing z as: $z = u^s - y^s = G(\hat{q}^a - q^a)$. Therefore, we have

$$\implies \|z\|_2 = \|G(\hat{q}^a - q^a)\|_2 \qquad (4.4.14)$$

$$= \|(\hat{q}^a - q^a)\|_2 \frac{\|G(\hat{q}^a - q^a)\|_2}{\|(\hat{q}^a - q^a)\|_2} \geq \|(\hat{q}^a - q^a)\|_2 \, \sigma_{\min}(G) \qquad (4.4.15)$$

Finally, by rearranging (4.4.15), we obtain the required statement

$$\|\hat{q}^a - q^a\|_2 \leq \frac{1}{\sigma_{\min}(G)} \|z\|_2 \qquad \qquad \square$$

Now, we see that if $\sigma_{\min}(G) \geq 1$, then the channel estimation error (measured using the l_2-norm) is smaller than or equal to the l_2-norm of the measurement error, i.e., $\|\hat{q}^a - q^a\|_2 \leq \|z\|_2$. This, in fact, is the case for the class of generator matrices introduced in the following proposition

Proposition 4.4.2. *Let I_m be the $m \times m$ identity matrix. Then, $\sigma_{min}(G) \geq 1$ for G of the form:*

$$G = \begin{pmatrix} I_m & P_{m \times n-m} \end{pmatrix} \qquad (4.4.16)$$

See Appendix B.3 for proof.

Remark 4.4.1.2. *It is not difficult to obtain generator matrices of the form in Eq. (4.4.16). For instance, syndrome source codes can be manipulated using row and column operations over the binary field to produce equivalent codes with G as in Eq. (4.4.16).*

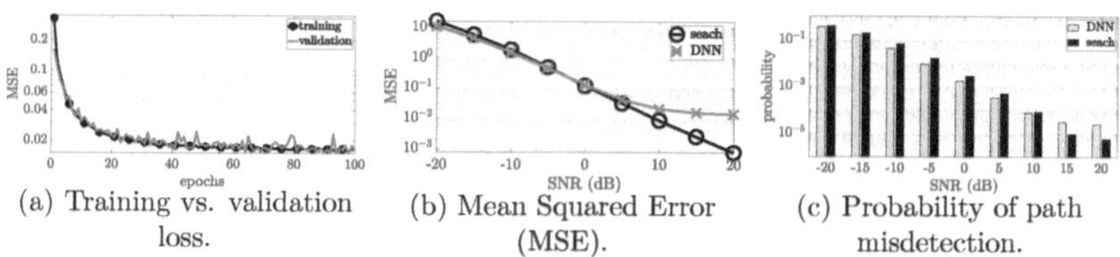

(a) Training vs. validation loss.

(b) Mean Squared Error (MSE).

(c) Probability of path misdetection.

Figure 4.3: Evaluation of DNN-based measurement to channel mapping.

4.5 Measurement Decoding

Designing channel measurements that have one-to-one correspondence with q^a is only part of the solution. Equally important, however, is the ability to "decode" y^s back to q^a, i.e., figuring out the function $\mathcal{D}(\cdot)$ in Eq. (4.3.1). The one-to-one correspondence between q^a and y^s guarantees that there exists an inverse function that maps y^s back to q^a. Nevertheless, since we can only obtain u^s; an error-corrupted version of y^s, we cannot exactly regenerate q^a, but rather, an estimate $\hat{q}^a$. Given that measurement errors occur, our objective is to obtain $\hat{q}^a$ such that its **distance** to q^a is as small as possible (i.e., minimize the estimation error). We use the l_2-norm as a distance measure between q^a and $\hat{q}^a$, defined as $\delta\left(q^a, \hat{q}^a\right) = \left\| q^a - \hat{q}^a \right\|_2$.

The problem of mapping the channel measurements to an estimated channel is non-linear and may require intensive computations. Two different methods to do this mapping were proposed in [55], namely, i) the "look-up table" method and ii) the "search" method. The look-up table method requires storing a table with entries for all possible channel measurements along with their corresponding channels. This is possible since measurements are quantized using ADCs and hence there exists a finite number of possibilities for y^s. However, the number of entries in the table could be quite large, especially, if high resolution ADCs are used. On the other hand, the search method requires a combinatorial search over the columns of $\boldsymbol{G}$ (recall that $\boldsymbol{y^s} \equiv \boldsymbol{G}\boldsymbol{q^a}$) for which the computational complexity is of order $O\left(n_r^k\right)$. This could be prohibitive for large antenna arrays. Motivated by the drawbacks of the look-up table and search methods, we propose an alternative *Machine Learning (ML)* based approach that uses *Deep Neural Networks (DNN)*.

4.5.1 DNN-based mapping

ML is widely used to solve very complex problems through *learning*. We focus on *supervised learning* to solve the decoding problem, which is a multi-dimensional non-linear regression problem for which neural networks is a powerful tool. Specifically, we use a fully connected classical DNN with an input layer of m nodes (equal to the measurement dimensions) and an output layer of n_r nodes (equal to the channel dimensions). The DNN model is designed to handle real-valued input-output data. But, on the contrary, both the channel $\boldsymbol{q^a}$ and measurements $\boldsymbol{y^s}$ are complex-valued. To overcome this problem, observe that $\boldsymbol{y^s}$ can be written as $\boldsymbol{y_R^s}+j\boldsymbol{y_I^s}$ and $\boldsymbol{q^a}$ as $\boldsymbol{q_R^a}+j\boldsymbol{q_I^a}$ (i.e., in terms of their real and imaginary components). And notice that $\boldsymbol{y_R^s}=\boldsymbol{G}\boldsymbol{q_R^a}$ and $\boldsymbol{y_I^s}=\boldsymbol{G}\boldsymbol{q_I^a}$. Therefore, we can construct an estimate $\boldsymbol{\hat{q}^a}$ using its real and imaginary components, i.e., $\boldsymbol{\hat{q}_R^a}+j\boldsymbol{\hat{q}_I^a}$, where $\boldsymbol{\hat{q}_R^a}$ and $\boldsymbol{\hat{q}_I^a}$ are estimated using $\boldsymbol{y_R^s}$ and $\boldsymbol{y_I^s}$ as inputs to the DNN model, respectively. Therefore, our DNN takes the measurement vectors $\boldsymbol{y^s}$ as inputs and produces the corresponding channel estimates $\boldsymbol{\hat{q}^a}$ at its output, but it does so in two different steps, handling the real and imaginary parts separately. For ease of notation, we will not use real and imaginary components to refer to inputs and outputs of the DNN models but it should be understood that this is how we handle it. The number of hidden layers and their corresponding number of nodes are design parameters that depend on the sizes of the input and output, and the relationship governing them. For all hidden layers, we use the rectified linear

(ReLU) activation function while for the output layer we use the linear activation function. We also use the *ADAM* optimizer [56] for training and the Mean Squared Error (MSE) loss function to quantify the model error[1].

Model training: Although we do not have a closed form expression for mapping $\boldsymbol{y}^s$ to $\boldsymbol{q}^a$ (hence the need for an algorithmic solution), generating training data is actually straightforward. This is because the reverse direction (i.e., mapping $\boldsymbol{q}^a$ to $\boldsymbol{y}^s$) is just a simple linear transformation. Training data is generated as follows: For every $\boldsymbol{q}_s^a \in \mathcal{Q}_s^a$ (recall that $\mathcal{Q}_s^a$ is the set of all possible channel support vectors defined in Section 4.4.2), we generate $n_s = 300$ random channels, $\boldsymbol{q}^a$, by choosing the non-zero components of $\boldsymbol{q}^a$ to be uniformly distributed in $[-\alpha_{\max}^b, \alpha_{\max}^b]$ where $\alpha_{\max}^b$ (recall Eq. (2.0.1)) is the maximum magnitude of baseband path gains, which can be obtained using channel statistics. Note that we can set $\alpha_{\max}^b$ to be the maximum ADC quantized value of $|\alpha_l^b|$. Thus, the total number of input-output samples we have is $n_s \times |\mathcal{Q}_s^a|$. We use 70% of these samples for training and the remaining 30% for validation. Training is done using 200 epochs with batches of size 32. We monitor the validation error to make sure that the model does not over-fit the training data. If over-fitting is observed (which is indicated by a persistent increase in validation error at the end of every epoch), we stop the training process and only keep the model which produced the least validation error. DNN training is done offline, and a trained DNN model is stored in memory to be used when needed.

4.5.2 DNN Model Assessment

To argue the reliability of DNN-based mapping, we test it using a channel with $n_t=1$, $n_r=23$ and a maximum of 3 paths i.e., $k \leq 3$. We compare its performance against

---

[1]We use Keras API [57] to build, train, test and use the DNN model we propose. Our pre-trained models and DNN-related codes are available in [58].

the "search" method of [55]. Based on the described channel parameters, only $m=11$ measurements are needed to discover its paths (more details about this particular example are discussed in Section 4.7). We design a DNN model with an input layer of $m=11$ nodes and an output layer of $n_r=23$ nodes. The model also has 5 hidden layers with $1024, 512, 512, 128$ and 128 nodes, respectively. We train the DNN model using data generated as described in Section 4.5.1. Fig. 4.3a shows the average MSE loss of both training and validation data sets for 100 epochs. Training achieves validation error of ≈ 0.0143 (averaged across all samples of validation data). The figure also shows close MSE values for training and validation. This indicates that the model generalizes well to measurements it had not seen before, which guarantees reliability for arbitrary measurements.

These initial results are promising. However, they are obtained using error-free measurements. This prompts us to test the resilience of DNN-based mapping against noisy measurements. We also compare its performance against the search method proposed in [55]. To do so, we generate a testing data set in the same way we created the training data. We also generate sets of uniformly distributed noise vectors where each noise set is drawn at a different value of transmit SNR from -20 to 20 dB. The noise vectors are then added to the inputs (channel measurements) of the testing data set then passed through the trained model. The decoded $\hat{q}^a$ is recorded at the output. Similarly, we use the "search" method to decode the same noise-corrupted measurements.

For evaluation, we use i) average MSE, as well as ii) the probability of path misdetection (i.e., no path discovery). We say a path is correctly discovered if the path gain of its corresponding component in $\hat{q}^a$ is among the $k=3$ strongest components in $\hat{q}^a$. Fig. 4.3b shows the average MSE obtained using the search and DNN-based mapping methods on a log scale. We see that at low SNR, DNN-based decoding outperforms the search method. This indicates that the DNN model is more resilient against measurement errors. At high SNR, however, the DNN's MSE saturates at ≈ 0.014 which is the same value we obtain for validation during model training using noise-free inputs (not that the MSE value at which DNN-based mapping saturates can be made lower by further improvement of the DNN model). The search method's MSE, on the other hand, keeps improving as SNR increases, nevertheless, for values below 10^{-2} the improvement is marginal. The probability of path misdetection, shown in Fig. 4.3c, confirms the performance trend of the MSE. Specifically, we see that at low SNR, the DNN-based model outperforms the search method (i.e., has lower probability of misdetection) while at high SNR we see that the search method is better.

Computational complexity: As we have previously discussed, the search method requires high computational power. Precisely, $\binom{n_r}{k}$ iterations with one matrix inversion and two matrix multiplication operations are performed per iteration, which then produces a vector of length m. Finally, an additional step of finding the minimum l_2−norm of all $\binom{n_r}{k}$ vectors is performed. On the other hand, the DNN-based mapping just requires N_k linear computations for the hidden and output layers, where N_k is the number of nodes at the kth layer. These computations are of the form $\sum_{i=1}^{N_{k-1}} w_i a_i$ where a_i is the value passed from the ith node of the previous layer and w_i is the weight on its link. For this particular example, the search method and the DNN-based method were implemented on the same machine and on average the search method's execution time was 11.2 ms compared to 47 μs for the DNN model.

4.6 Multiple Transmit and Receive Antennas

So far, we only dealt with channels of single-transmit, multiple-receive antennas. Recall that this setting is almost identical to multiple-transmit, single-receive antenna

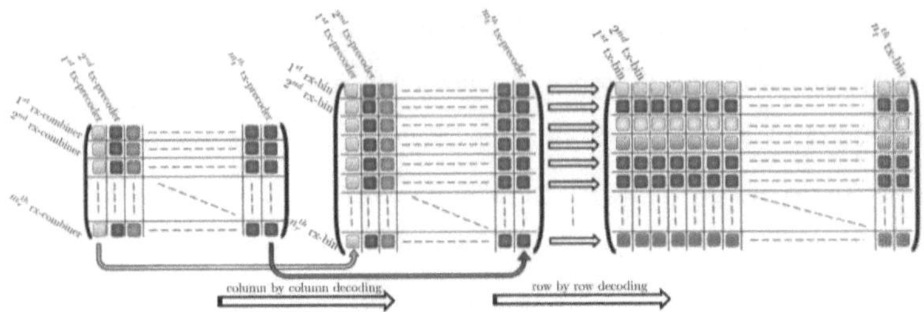

Figure 4.4: Measurement decoding for channels with multiple TX/RX antennas is done in two steps. Given the matrix $\boldsymbol{Y^s}$ whose $y^s_{i,j}th$ component is $= \boldsymbol{w}_i^H \boldsymbol{Q} \boldsymbol{f}_j$ (shown on the left), we first do a column by column decoding where the jth decoded column of $\boldsymbol{Y^s}$ is $\boldsymbol{q}^a_{rx,j}$. Then, in the second step we decode the intermediary matrix row by row to produce $\hat{\boldsymbol{Q}}^a$ (shown on the right). The two decoding functions of first and second steps are dependent on the source codes used to design $\boldsymbol{w_i}$'s and $\boldsymbol{f_j}$'s, respectively.

channels, except that in the former setting we seek to design $\boldsymbol{w_i}$'s to estimate the angular channel at RX, while in the latter, we design $\boldsymbol{f_j}$'s to estimate the angular channel at TX. In this section, we extend the channel setting to be of **_multiple-transmit, multiple-receive_** antennas. We build on the design principles and decoding methods of single transmit antenna channels and show how measurements are obtained and decoded to estimate the entire $n_r \times n_t$ channel.

4.6.1   Measurements

Unlike the single transmit antenna scenario where TX sends signals omnidirectionally, it can now focus its transmission on narrow angular directions. However, from RX's point of view, no matter which set of directions the TX is transmitting into, it can only see a number of n_r resolvable bins; only k of which may have paths to TX. The same is true from TX's perspective, where the TX can only see n_t resolvable bins, only k of which may have paths to the receiver[2]. Thus, for an arbitrary tx-precoder, the receiver would need to measure the channel using the same set of $\boldsymbol{w_i}$'s it needs for the $n_t = 1$ setting. Upon decoding, the result would be n_r angular rx bins (corresponding to the particular $\boldsymbol{f_j}$ used at TX). Similarly, for an arbitrary rx-combiner, the transmitter would need the same set of $\boldsymbol{f_j}$'s it needs for the $n_r = 1$ setting to find its respective tx bins. To find such $\boldsymbol{f_j}$'s and $\boldsymbol{w_i}$'s, we invoke Theorem 4.4.1.

Let $\boldsymbol{f_j}$ $\forall j \in \{1, \ldots, m_t\}$ be the tx-precoding vectors and $\boldsymbol{w_i}$ $\forall i \in \{1, \ldots, m_r\}$ be the rx-combining vectors. Then, the channel measurements are obtained as follows: The transmitter sends a number of m_r pilot symbols using **each** of its m_t precoders. On the receiver side, for every tx-precoder, m_r channel measurements are obtained using the distinct m_r rx-combiners. Recall that $u_{i,j} = y_{i,j}^s + \boldsymbol{w}_i^H \boldsymbol{n}$ where $y_{i,j}^s = \boldsymbol{w}_i^H \boldsymbol{Q} \boldsymbol{f}_j$ (see Eq. (2.0.8)). Let us arrange the m_r measurements corresponding to the jth tx-precoder in $\boldsymbol{y}_j^s$ and define $\boldsymbol{Y}^s$ as

$$\boldsymbol{Y}^s \triangleq \begin{pmatrix} \boldsymbol{y}_1^s & \boldsymbol{y}_2^s & \cdots & \boldsymbol{y}_{m_t}^s \end{pmatrix}. \tag{4.6.1}$$

Thus, $\boldsymbol{Y}^s$ contains all $m_t \times m_r$ channel measurements necessary to discover all available paths.

---

[2]Recall that the directions at which the TX is transmitting and the RX is receiving are determined by their antenna beam patterns which are in turn determined by $\boldsymbol{f_j}$ and $\boldsymbol{w_i}$, respectively (see Fig. 4.2).

4.6.2 Decoding Y^s

To obtain $\hat{Q}^a$ from Y^s, we perform multiple SIMO decoding operations[3], as described in Section 4.5. This procedure is highlighted in the diagram in Fig. 4.4 and is detailed as follows:

(i) Decode every y_j^s $\forall j\{1, 2, \ldots, m_t\}$ to obtain $q_{rx,j}^a$. Recall that y_j^s is the measurement vector corresponding to the jth tx-precoder. Thus, $q_{rx,j}^a$, is the $n_r \times 1$ mm-wave channel observed at RX due to the TX signal transmission through the angular directions featured by f_j.

(ii) After Step (i), we obtain a sequence of m_t "measurement" components corresponding to each rx-bin. Each of these components is produced using a distinct tx-precoder. Let us denote these sequences by $y_{tx,k}^s$ ($1 \times m_t$ row vectors), where $k \in \{1, 2, \ldots, n_r\}$.

(iii) Decode each $y_{tx,k}^s$ to obtain $q_{tx,k}^a$ ($1 \times n_t$ row vectors) whose components constitute all the tx-bins corresponding to the kth rx-bin.

(iv) Stack all $q_{tx,k}^a$ to obtain $\hat{Q}^a$ (each representing the kth row of $\hat{Q}^a$).

4.7 Performance Evaluation

We evaluate the performance of our proposed coding-based solution under various simulation scenarios. Specifically, we consider 23×23 and 15×32 multi-path channels.

---

[3] Alternatively, we could have trained a large DNN model which accepts all measurements Y^s and outputs an estimate $\hat{Q}^a$. Adopting this strategy, however, results in overwhelming training complexity since this model would need to be trained with a massive training data set of size $n_s \times |\mathcal{Q}_s^a| = n_s \sum_{i=0}^{k} \binom{n_r \times n_t}{i}$, where $\mathcal{Q}_s^a$ now is the set of all support vectors of size $n_r n_t \times 1$ that represent the $n_r \times n_t$ vectorized channel matrices. Compare this to our solution of using 2 DNN models trained with data sets of sizes $n_s \sum_{i=0}^{k} \binom{n_r}{i}$ and $n_s \sum_{i=0}^{k} \binom{n_t}{i}$, respectively.

For both channel settings, we assume the existence of a maximum of 3 paths[4]. We also consider 15×31 single-path channels. The single-path assumption is appropriate for LoS scenarios where the path gain of the LoS is significantly higher than the gains of Non-LoS (NLoS) paths (≈ 20 dB higher [3]).

To understand how our solution compares to the state-of-the-art, we implement a compressed-sensing-based channel estimation solution, as well as the IEEE 802.11ad's (WiGig) beam discovery method. Note that, while compressed sensing is a generic solution that can be applied to multi-path channels (similar to our solution), the WiGig method is designed to discover one channel path, hence, we only use it for the 15×31 single-path channel. Our results demonstrate that our proposed solution is more resilient to errors compared to both CS and 802.11ad, and produces higher quality estimates. Furthermore, we study the effect of ADC resolution on channel estimation performance. This is important because ADC's power consumption is directly proportional to their resolution. Hence, it is necessary to understand the resolution limit beyond which only minimal gains, in terms of channel estimation performance, can be achieved.

4.7.1 Performance Metrics

We adopt performance metrics that highlight: (i) the measurement overhead, (ii) accuracy of path discovery (iii) quality of the estimated path gains, and (iv) the impact of the channel estimates on achievable data rate. These metrics are evaluated numerically, using Monte Carlo simulations (averaged over 10^5 simulation runs) and evaluated against different values of SNR. We define the performance metrics as follows: *i) Number of measurements*: Given by $m_t \times m_r$. *ii) Probability of path discovery:* Paths are said to exist at the strongest L components in the

---

[4]Note that information on L can be obtained from statistical channel models [3,59].

estimated channel $\hat{Q}^a$. ***iii) MSE*** (Normalized): Defined as the squared value of the Frobenius-norm of the estimation error, $Q^a - \hat{Q}^a$, normalized by the Frobenius-norm of Q^a, i.e., $\dfrac{\left\| Q^a - \hat{Q}^a \right\|_F^2}{\|Q^a\|_F^2}$. ***iv) Outage Rate***: Denoted by R_{out} and defined as $R_{\text{out}} \triangleq \mathbb{E}\left[\left(1 - \mathbb{1}_{\{\text{out}\}}\right) \times C_{Q}\right]$ where C_{Q} is the MIMO channel capacity of the channel Q [48], and $\mathbb{1}_{\{\text{out}\}}$ is the indicator function that takes a value of 1 in case of outage and 0 otherwise. We assume that an outage occurs if any of the strong channel paths were misdetected.

4.7.2 Implemented Solutions

1- Source Coding: We test three different measurement decoding methods, which we integrate with our coding-based solution. All three methods are used to solve each of the sub-problems depicted in Fig. (4.4). The first is the "search" method of [55]. The second and third decoding methods are based on DNNs, but they differ in the way they are trained, i.e., with or without measurement errors. We explain them as follows:

- **DNN**: Here, DNN models are trained using pure measurements, with no added noise components. Since models are not trained with errors, only one model can be used at all SNR and ADC resolution levels.

- **DNN-sd**: Since measurement errors tend to degrade the performance of path discovery, we try to overcome this impediment by training DNN models with error-corrupted measurements. Since errors are dependent on ADC resolution and SNR (see Eq. (2.0.7)), we train multiple DNNs for different values of each. We call such model "DNN with selective defense" or "DNN-sd". Note that the DNN-sd model is not dependent on specific path gain values since our SNR

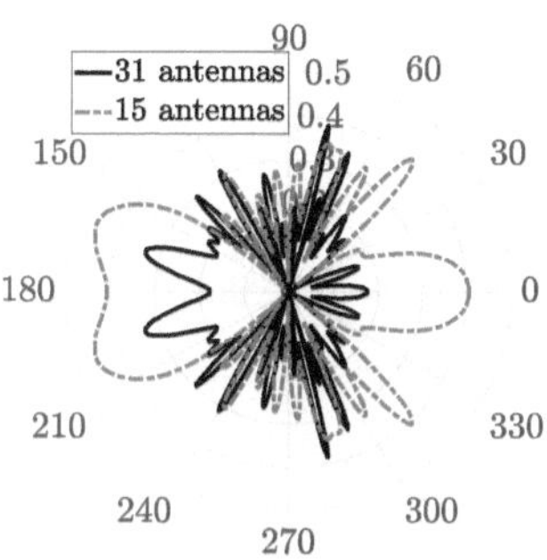

Figure 4.5: Antenna pattern example using CS.

definition does not include the effect of individual path gains α_l and because training is done using a wide range of uniformly distributed path gain values.

The DNN model parameters, including the number of layers, the number of nodes (neurons) per layer and the activation function, are selected using cross-validation. We also select the DNN model's size such that we have a reasonably good input-output mapping performance while keeping the processing speed fairly fast. We used `tensorflow` [60] for creating and using DNN models. ***Both types of DNN models are trained offline and stored in memory.***

2- Compressed Sensing: We use a similar formulation for the mmWave channel estimation problem as in [27, 28]. The tx-precoders and rx-combiners are obtained using random, uniformly distributed phase shift values. That is, the components of all $\boldsymbol{f_j}$'s and $\boldsymbol{w_i}$'s are of the form $\exp(j\vartheta)$ where $\vartheta \sim [0, 2\pi)$. Fig. 4.5 shows antenna pattern examples for random beamforming with 15 and 31 antennas. For measurement decoding, we use the "search" method, which is the optimal l_0-norm minimization solution [16] for solving each of the sub-problems of channel decoding. While this may still be too computationally complex to be of practical use, it provides an upper bound on the performance of other forms of sparse recovery algorithms like OMP, l_1 and l_2-norm minimization, etc.

3- 802.11ad: We only consider the Sector Level Sweep stage of the channel estimation scheme of 802.11ad. At this stage, the TX starts by sequentially transmitting packets in all possible transmit AoDs (sectors) while the receiver performs quasi omni-directional reception. Then, the TX and RX switch modes where TX forms a quasi omni-directional pattern while RX sweeps through all possible receive AoAs (sectors). The directions that reveal the highest received signal strength is denoted as the AoA and AoD of the strongest channel path.

4.7.3 Equating Energy Consumption

Various channel estimation solutions may require different number of measurements and may have different beamforming gains. Thus, it would not be fair to compare them at fixed transmission power. Instead, it is more fair to fix the total energy consumption for the whole channel estimation process of each solution. Thus, for comparison purposes, we opt to adjust the transmit power of each scheme such that *the total amount of energy consumption for the entire measurement process remains the same*.

Energy Calculation: The energy consumption, denoted by E_T, is given by $E_T = m \times P_T \times \tau$, where m is the number of measurements, P_T is the total transmit power per measurement and τ is the time duration of one measurement. Since the antenna patterns at TX/RX of our proposed scheme consist of multiple overlapped beams (recall Fig. 4.2), the total power P_T is an integer multiple of the transmit power per direction/beam P, which depends on the number of overlapped beams at TX and RX. Let o_t and o_r denote the number of overlapped beams at the TX and RX, respectively. Hence, we have that $P_T = o_t \times o_r \times P$. We can further write the transmit power per beam as $P = \text{SNR}\dfrac{N_0}{\mu}$ (recall Eq. (2.0.7)). This gives us a total energy consumption (in millijoules (mJ)) for the entire measurement process as: $E_T = m \times o_t \times o_r \times \text{SNR}\dfrac{N_0}{\mu} \times \tau$. Let $\mu = -88\text{dB}$ and $N_0 = 88\text{dBm}$[5]. Finally, let $\tau \approx 23\mu s$ (from IEEE 802.11ad).

4.7.4 Results

15×31 **single-path channels:** For this scenario, we choose ADCs of resolution $b{=}6$ bits. We provide results for our coding-based solution with both search and DNN-sd decoding. We also provide results for compressed sensing with search-based decoding, and IEEE 802.11ad beam alignment. We plot the results against the consumed energy E_T. **Source code selection:** We choose codes which satisfy the requirements in Theorem 4.4.1 as follows: At the TX side, we choose the $(31, 26)$ Hamming code to design tx-precoders, while at the RX side we choose the $(15, 11)$ Hamming code to design rx-combiners. Both of which operate as syndrome source codes with generator matrices $\boldsymbol{G_t}$ and $\boldsymbol{G_r}$ of sizes 5×31 and 4×15, respectively. Hence, we have $m_t{=}5$ and $m_r{=}4$, which gives us a **total number of 20 measurements**. For compressed sensing, we use the same number of measurements (i.e., $m = 20$). An exhaustive search, on the other hand, requires 465 measurements (our solution represents a measurement 95% reduction), while the IEEE 802.11ad scheme requires 46 measurements (57% reduction).

---

[5]To find μ and N_0, we assume a channel operating at a carrier frequency $f_c{=}60$ GHz with bandwidth $B{=}100$ MHz and distance between TX/RX of $d{=}10$m. Further, we assume a receiver system with noise figure NF $=6$ dB and temperature $T_0{=}293°$ kelvin. The path loss constitutes both the free space path loss (FSPL) and atmospheric absorption. FSPL is given as: $\text{FSPL} = -10\log_{10}\left(\dfrac{4\pi}{c}df_c\right)^{n_p}$, where $n_p{=}2$ is the path loss exponent. Atmospheric absorption, however, can be ignored for small distances (≤ 50m) [61]. Hence, $\mu{=}\text{FSPL} = -88\text{dB}$. The noise power (in dBm) can be given as $N_0{=}10\log_{10}\left(k_B T_0 B \times 1000\right) + \text{NF}$, where k_B is the Boltzmann constant.

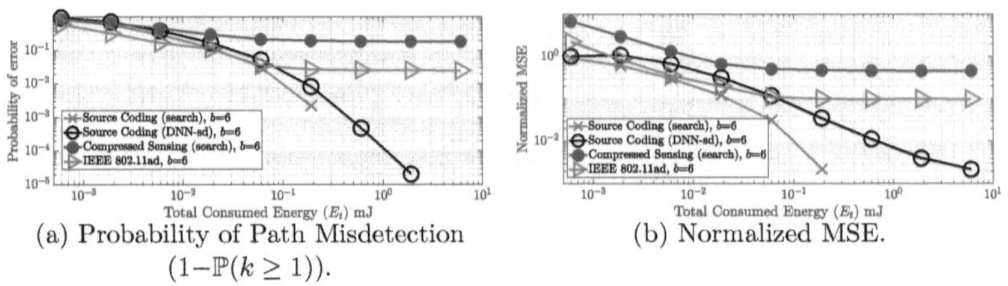

(a) Probability of Path Misdetection
$(1-\mathbb{P}(k \geq 1))$.

(b) Normalized MSE.

Figure 4.6: Performance of single-path 15×31 channels.

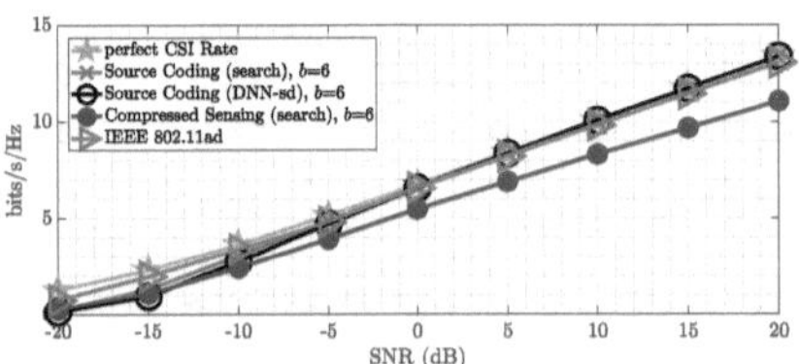

Figure 4.7: Outage Rate (R_{out}) of single-path 15×31 channels.

For the source coding method, both the normalized MSE and probability of path misdirection results, shown in Fig. 4.6, depict that DNN-sd decoding has a slightly worse performance compared to the search method. This is a small sacrifice in performance that is traded for a huge advantage in processing speed. The IEEE 802.11ad's method shows superior performance at low E_T (below 0.1 mJ). As E_T increases, however, its performance seizes to improve, while our source coding solution keeps approaching perfect channel discovery. When examining the outage rate, in Fig. 4.7, we see that the relatively high MSE error and probability of path misdetection of 802.11ad, does not result in a significant degradation in R_{out}. In fact, it has very close value to the perfect CSI capacity. Recall that 802.11ad requires almost twice the number of channel measurements. The compressed sensing method, on the other

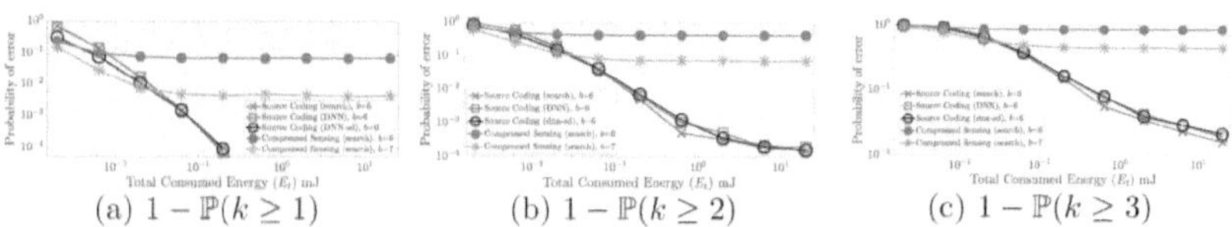

(a) $1 - \mathbb{P}(k \geq 1)$ (b) $1 - \mathbb{P}(k \geq 2)$ (c) $1 - \mathbb{P}(k \geq 3)$

Figure 4.8: Beam detection probability of error for 23×23 channels with $L \leq 3$.

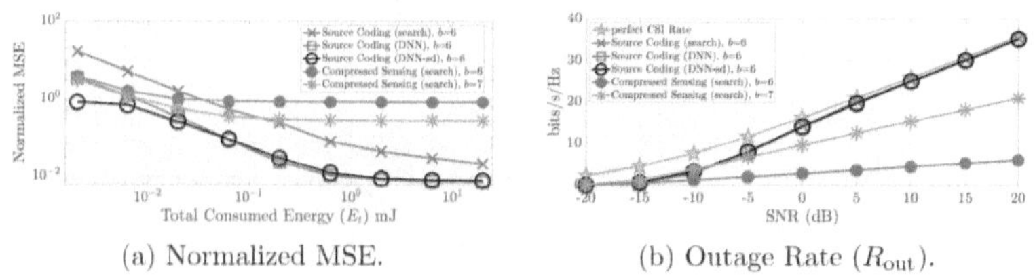

(a) Normalized MSE.   (b) Outage Rate (R_{out}).

Figure 4.9: MSE and Outage Rate for 23×23 channels with $L \leq 3$.

hand, has the lowest R_{out} and the highest MSE and probability of path misdetection among all other schemes.

23×23 **multi-path channels:** This is a more challenging multi-path scenario where, in addition to the previous solutions, we also investigate the performance of DNN decoding for which training is done with pure uncorrupted measurements. **Source code selection:** For this channel, since $n_r = n_t$, the same source code works for designing both tx-precoders and rx-combiners. The ***perfect binary Golay code*** used as a syndrome source code is a suitable choice for this problem. It has a generator matrix of size 11×22, hence, we have $m_t = m_r = 11$, and the **total number of required channel measurements is** $m_t \times m_r = 121$. Compared to the exhaustive search approach, which requires scanning all 529 combinations of TX/RX angular directions, this represents **75%** measurement reduction. For compressed sensing, we use the same number of precoders and combiners, as well.

First, for the probability of path detection, shown in Fig. 4.8, we notice very close performance for all three measurement decoding methods (search, DNN and DNN-sd) when integrated with our source coding solution. This suggests that DNNs are very efficient. And, while DNN-sd has a slight edge over DNN, the improvement is not significant. Hence, it is possible to user fewer DNNs trained over larger ranges of error components. Interestingly, however, in Fig. 4.9a, we observe that the search decoding of our source-coding-based measurements tend to have significantly larger MSE. This indicates that DNNs tend to suppress the error components in the estimated channel values, even though the correct channel paths may not be efficiently discovered. This is an artifact of DNN training which suggests that we may be able to improve the DNN's decoding performance if they were directly trained to discover the channel paths rather than just decrease the MSE of the channel estimates.

Compressed sensing, however has significantly worse performance in terms of path discover, MSE and outage Rate. At very low E_T, CS's performance improves as E_T gets higher, but at $E_T \geq 0.7$ the improvement stops. This suggests that the CS-based solution is more sensitive to quantification error. This is verified by using a higher resolution ADC ($b=7$ bits) which shows a significant improvement of performance.

15×32 **multi-path channel:** The performance results under this scenario is very similar to the 23×23 channel setting shown above. Specifically, Fig. 4.10 shows the probability of path discovery where our coding method with search decoding shows superior performance compared to DNN-sd decoding. On the contrary, search has worse MSE compared to DNN-sd (as shown in Fig.4.11a). Compressed sensing, has close performance to our proposed solution at low E_T. At high E_T, however, its performance only sees marginal improvement, unlike our proposed solution which keeps approaching perfect channel discovery. **Code selection:** We choose codes whose

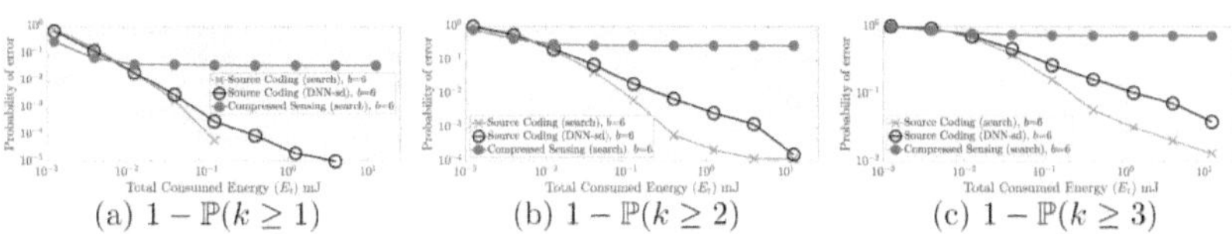

(a) $1 - \mathbb{P}(k \geq 1)$ (b) $1 - \mathbb{P}(k \geq 2)$ (c) $1 - \mathbb{P}(k \geq 3)$

Figure 4.10: Beam detection probability of error for 15×32 channels with $L \leq 3$.

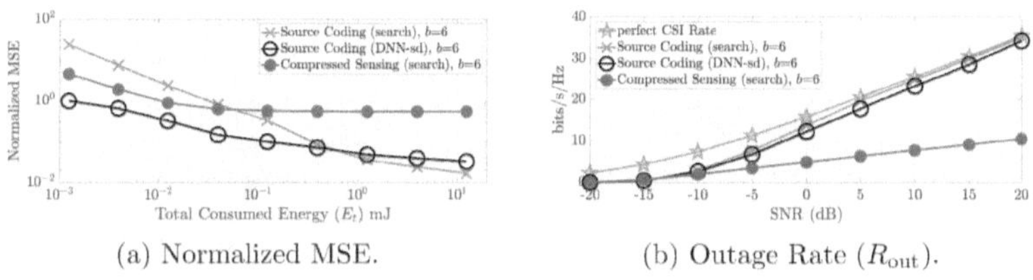

(a) Normalized MSE.   (b) Outage Rate (R_{out}).

Figure 4.11: MSE and Outage Rate for 15×32 channels with $L \leq 3$.

$m_r = 11$ and $m_t = 16$. The **total number of required channel measurements is** 176, which constitutes 63.3% measurement reduction compared to exhaustive search.

4.7.5 Effect of ADC resolution on performance:

Now, we provide and compare results for 23×23 channels with ADCs of b=3, 5, and 7−bit resolution, inas well as the ideal $b = \infty$. We only show results for DNN-sd decoding since the performance of the other two methods compare similarly to the trends of the ideal ADC case shown above. In Fig. 4.12a, we plot the MSE. As expected, we see that MSE is inversely proportional to resolution. We can also see that as SNR increases, higher resolution is required to keep the MSE close to that of ideal ADCs. For instance, b=5 is reasonably good up to SNR $= -5$dB, while b=7 is very close to $b=\infty$ up to SNR $= 5$dB. Even at high SNR, the b=7 curve has a gap with ideal ADCs that is smaller than 5×10^{-3}. Similar performance trend is exhibited

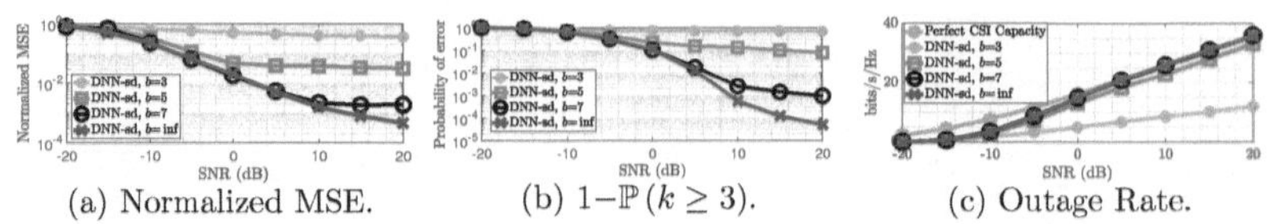

(a) Normalized MSE.   (b) $1-\mathbb{P}\left(k \geq 3\right)$.   (c) Outage Rate.

Figure 4.12: Performance of various ADC quantizations.

for the probability of path discovery, shown in Fig. 4.12b. Finally, the outage rate is depicted in Fig. 4.12c. We see that $b{=}7$ results in R_{out} that is almost identical to that of the ideal ADC, and that both of which are very close to the perfect CSI capacity. We also see that at low SNR, there is a considerable gap between the perfect CSI capacity and outage rate even for ideal ADCs.

4.8   Conclusion

In this work, we treat the mmWave channel estimation problem a source compression problem. Our goal is to reconstruct the channel matrix using a small number of measurements. We exploit linear binary source codes for encoding the channel (do measurements) and a deep neural network based algorithm for measurement decoding (channel reconstruction). We are able, using a small number of measurements, to obtain high quality channel estimates. The lower bound on the achievable number of measurements is accurately characterized. Through simulation, the superiority of our proposed solution is demonstrated, in comparison to compressed-sensing-based solutions and IEEE 802.11ad's beam alignment.

CHAPTER 5

BASIC LIMITS

5.1 Introduction

While numerous solutions, including **Compressed Sensing** (CS) [47, 62], have been used for mmWave channel estimation in order to reduce the number of measurements, it remains unclear as to what is the relationship between the smallest number of measurements and the channel structure (i.e., the channel dimensions and its sparsity level). The closest effort to understanding how changing the number of measurements affects the quality of channel estimates, to the best of our knowledge, is [27], where computer simulations were conducted to measure the quality of channel estimates as the number of measurements increases. Nonetheless, there is still a gap in the current literature in understanding the *lower bound* on the number of necessary measurements needed for accurate channel recovery. To the best of our knowledge, the tightest known bound scales as $\Omega\left(k \log \frac{n_t n_r}{k}\right)$ [9, 16], where k is the channel sparsity level and n_t and n_r are the numbers of antennas at TX and RX, respectively. This bound, however, is a naive application of the CS bound for recovery of sparse vectors of length $n = n_t n_r$ and k non-zero values. In fact, the nature of the channel estimation problem poses limitations on how measurements are obtained, as opposed to the standard CS problem. More precisely, the sensing matrix used for MIMO channel estimation has a Kronecker product form and is function of both the beamforming vectors and the linear transform dictionary matrices used for representing the channel in a sparse domain. Thus, more attention needs to be paid when deriving measurement lower bounds. The optimal choice of beamforming vectors and the dictionary matrices that would produce optimal sensing matrices, to best of our knowledge, has not been studied yet. In this chapter, we show that the aforementioned bound is too loose, and we provide a tighter lower bound which has order of $\Omega\left(k^2 \log\left(\frac{n_t}{k}\right)\log\left(\frac{n_r}{k}\right)\right)$. We argue the tightness of this bound by showing that, under a mild constraint on the channel sparsity level, there exists a solution with a number of measurements upper bounded as $O(k^2 \log\left(\frac{n_t}{k}\right)\log\left(\frac{n_r}{k}\right))$.

5.2   Lower Measurement Bounds

While numerous solutions, including **Compressed Sensing** (CS) [47, 62], have been used for mmWave channel estimation in order to reduce the number of measurements, it remains unclear as to what is the relationship between the smallest number of measurements and the channel structure (i.e., the channel dimensions and its sparsity level). The closest effort to understanding how changing the number of measurements affects the quality of channel estimates, to the best of our knowledge, is [27], where computer simulations were conducted to measure the quality of channel estimates as the number of measurements increases. Nonetheless, there is still a gap in the current literature in understanding the *lower bound* on the number of necessary measurements needed for accurate channel recovery. To the best of our knowledge, the tightest known bound scales as $\Omega\left(k \log \frac{n_t n_r}{k}\right)$ [9, 16], where k is the channel sparsity level and n_t and n_r are the numbers of antennas at TX and RX, respectively. This bound, however, is a naive application of the CS bound for recovery of sparse vectors of length $n = n_t n_r$ and k non-zero values. In fact, the nature of the channel estimation problem poses limitations on how measurements are obtained, as opposed to the standard CS problem. More precisely, the sensing matrix used for MIMO channel estimation has a Kronecker product form and is function of both the beamforming vectors and the linear transform dictionary matrices used for representing the channel in a sparse domain. Thus, more attention needs to be paid when deriving measurement lower bounds. The optimal choice of beamforming vectors and the dictionary matrices that would produce optimal sensing matrices, to best of our knowledge, has not been studied yet. In this chapter, we show that the aforementioned bound is too loose, and we provide a tighter lower bound which has order of $\Omega\left(k^2 \log\left(\frac{n_t}{k}\right) \log\left(\frac{n_r}{k}\right)\right)$. We argue the tightness of this bound by showing that, under a mild constraint on the channel sparsity level, there exists a solution with a number of measurements upper bounded as $O(k^2 \log\left(\frac{n_t}{k}\right) \log\left(\frac{n_r}{k}\right))$.

5.3   Problem Formulation

In this section, we will provide a brief overview of compressed sensing (CS). Then, we will formulate the problem of channel estimation as a CS problem. To that end, we will reshape the measurement equation given in Eq. (2.0.9) to be in the form $\boldsymbol{y}_v = \boldsymbol{G}_v \boldsymbol{q}_v^a + \boldsymbol{n}_v$, which conforms with the traditional compressed sensing problem, as will be shown in Eq. (5.3.1) below. Here, $\boldsymbol{q}_v^a$ is sparse and has dimensions $n_r n_t \times 1$.

5.3.1   Compressed Sensing Background

Compressed sensing is a signal processing technique [62] that allows the reconstruction of a signal $\boldsymbol{x} = (x_i)_{i=1}^n$ from a small number of samples *given that* $\boldsymbol{x}$ is either: (i) sparse, or (ii) can be represented in a sparse form, using a linear transformation $\boldsymbol{U}$ such that $\boldsymbol{x} = \boldsymbol{U}\boldsymbol{s}$ where $\boldsymbol{s}$ is sparse. Let the number of measurements be denoted by m where $m < n$ and $m, n \in \mathbb{N}$. Each measurement of $\boldsymbol{x}$ is a linear combination of its components x_i. Such measurements are dictated by the sensing matrix $\boldsymbol{G}$ and are given by $\boldsymbol{y} = \boldsymbol{G}\boldsymbol{x}$, where $\boldsymbol{y}$ denotes the $m{\times}1$ measurement vector. The matrix equation $\boldsymbol{y} = \boldsymbol{G}\boldsymbol{x}$ represents an under-determined system of linear equations (since $m < n$). In other words, we have fewer equations than the number of unknowns we want to solve for. While, in general, an infinite number of solutions exist, the sparsity of $\boldsymbol{x}$ allows for perfect signal reconstruction from $\boldsymbol{y}$ *given that* certain conditions are satisfied, among which, is a lower bound on the "*spark*" of the sensing matrix.

Definition 5.3.1. *The spark of a given matrix $\boldsymbol{G}$ is the smallest number of its linearly dependent columns.*

Theorem 5.3.1 (Corollary 1 of [63]). *For any vector $\boldsymbol{y} \in \mathbb{R}^m$, there exits at most one vector $\boldsymbol{q}^a \in \mathbb{R}^n$ with $\|\boldsymbol{q}^a\|_0 = k$ such that $\boldsymbol{y} = \boldsymbol{G}\boldsymbol{q}^a$ if and only if* $\mathrm{spark}(\boldsymbol{G}) > 2k$.

Theorem 5.3.1 provides a mathematical guarantee on the exact recovery of $k-$sparse vectors using m linear measurements. An immediate bound on the number of measurements, m, we get from Theorem 5.3.1 is $m \geq 2k$. The lower bound on the spark of $\boldsymbol{G}$ works well under noise-free measurements, but in practice, measurements get corrupted with a vector $\boldsymbol{n}$, i.e.,

$$\boldsymbol{y} = \boldsymbol{G}\boldsymbol{x} + \boldsymbol{n}. \tag{5.3.1}$$

It is necessary to guarantee that the measurement process is not adversely affected by such errors in a significant way. This calls for alternative, stricter requirements on sensing matrices to guarantee "good" sparse recovery. Mathematically, we need to design the sensing matrix such that the energy in the measured signal is preserved. This is quantified using the **Restricted Isometry Property (RIP)**. The RIP property guarantees that the distance between any pair of $k-$sparse vectors is not significantly changed under the measurement process. This RIP property is defined as follows:

Definition 5.3.2. *A matrix $\boldsymbol{G}$ satisfies the restricted isometry property (RIP) of order k if there exists a constant $\delta_k \in (0,1)$ such that for all vectors $\boldsymbol{q^a}$, with $\|\boldsymbol{q^a}\|_0 \leq k$, we have*

$$(1 - \delta_k) \|\boldsymbol{q^a}\|_2^2 \leq \|\boldsymbol{G q^a}\|_2^2 \leq (1 + \delta_k) \|\boldsymbol{q^a}\|_2^2 . \tag{5.3.2}$$

The smallest δ_k which satisfies Eq. (5.3.2) is called the "$k-$restricted isometry constant". Note that in general, a matrix $\tilde{\boldsymbol{G}}$ does not necessarily result in $\|\tilde{\boldsymbol{G}} \boldsymbol{q^a}\|^2$ that is symmetric about 1. However, a simple scaling of $\tilde{\boldsymbol{G}}$ results in $\boldsymbol{G}$ such that the tightest bounds of $\|\boldsymbol{G q^a}\|^2$ in Eq. (5.3.2) are symmetric [64]. From now on, we will only consider matrices whose bounds are symmetric as shown in Eq. (5.3.2).

The following theorem provides a necessary condition for $m \times n$ matrices that satisfy the RIP property with $\delta_k \in (0,1)$.

Theorem 5.3.2 (Theorem 3.5 of [65]). *Let $\boldsymbol{G}$ be an $m \times n$ matrix that satisfies RIP of order k with constant $\delta_k \in (0,1)$. Then,*

$$m \geq c_\delta k \log \left(\frac{n}{k} \right) \tag{5.3.3}$$

where $c_\delta = \dfrac{0.18}{\log \left(\sqrt{\frac{1+\delta}{1-\delta}} + 1 \right)}$, is a function of δ only.

Theorem 5.3.2 demonstrates the popular asymptotic measurement bound: $m = \Omega \left(k \log \frac{n}{k} \right)$. Next, we will formulate the MIMO channel estimation as a compressed sensing problem.

5.3.2 The Problem

Recall from Eq. (2.0.9) that channel measurements take the form

$$Y = W^H Q F + N.$$

This is not the standard form of a noisy CS problem (see Eq. (5.3.1)). Thus, it cannot readily be solved using compressed sensing. To put this equation in a CS problem form, let us *"vectorize"* its left and right hand sides as follows:

- Let $y_v = \text{vec}(Y)$

- Let $n_v = \text{vec}(N)$

- And by the properties of *vectorization* [66], we have

$$
\begin{aligned}
\text{vec}(W^H Q F) &= (F^T \otimes W^H)\,\text{vec}(Q) & (5.3.4)\\
&= (F^T \otimes W^H)\,\text{vec}(U_r Q^a U_t^H) & (5.3.5)\\
&= (F^T \otimes W^H)(U_t^* \otimes U_r)\,\text{vec}(Q^a) & (5.3.6)\\
&= (F^T \otimes W^H)(U_t^* \otimes U_r)\,q_v^a & (5.3.7)\\
&= ((F^T U_t^*) \otimes (W^H U_r))\,q_v^a & (5.3.8)\\
&= \left((F^H U_t)^* \otimes (W^H U_r)\right) q_v^a & (5.3.9)
\end{aligned}
$$

Thus, we can rewrite the measurement equation in (2.0.9) as

$$y_v = G_v q_v^a + n_v, \tag{5.3.10}$$

$$\textit{where} \quad G_v = \left(F^H U_t\right)^* \otimes \left(W^H U_r\right) \tag{5.3.11}$$

is the sensing matrix, with dimensions $m_t m_r \times n_t n_r$, while y_v has dimensions $m_t m_r \times 1$ and q_v^a has dimensions $n_t n_r \times 1$. This form of the problem allows us to employ CS sparse recovery techniques to estimate q_v^a from y_v.

5.4   Lower Measurement Bound

We are interested in sensing matrices that preserve the ***distance*** between two different channels $\boldsymbol{q}_{v1}^{a}$ and $\boldsymbol{q}_{v2}^{a}$. This distance is the norm of $\boldsymbol{q}_{v1}^{a} - \boldsymbol{q}_{v2}^{a}$, which has a sparsity level of $2k$ (recall that the maximum number of channel paths is k). Thus, to be able to accurately estimate $\boldsymbol{q}_{v}^{a}$, we need the sensing matrix $\boldsymbol{G}_{v}$ to satisfy the RIP property of order $2k$ with some RIP constant $\delta_{2k} \in (0,1)$. At sparsity level of $2k$, Theorem 5.3.2 shows that the recovery of a sparse vector with dimensions $n=n_t n_r$ requires a number of measurements, m, lower bounded as

$$m \geq c_\delta (2k) \log \left(\frac{n_t n_r}{(2k)} \right) \tag{5.4.1}$$

$$= 2c_\delta k \left(\log \left(\frac{n_t}{\sqrt{2k}} \right) + \log \left(\frac{n_r}{\sqrt{2k}} \right) \right). \tag{5.4.2}$$

This demonstrates the popular $m = \Omega \left(k \log \left(\frac{n_r \times n_t}{k} \right) \right)$ lower bound for sparse channel estimation. Although this bound is valid, it is in fact too loose since it assumes that arbitrary constructions of $\boldsymbol{G}_{v}$ are possible. This, however, is not the case for sparse MIMO channel estimation since $\boldsymbol{G}_{v}$ takes a special, Kronecker product form, as derived in Eq. (5.3.11).

Next, we will derive a tighter bound on the number of measurements. A bound that considers the special structure of the sensing matrix. This will result in $m = \Omega \left(k^2 \log \left(\frac{n_t}{k} \right) \log \left(\frac{n_r}{k} \right) \right)$. To appreciate how much tighter our derived bound is, we plot the functions $k \log \left(\frac{n_t \times n_r}{k} \right)$ and $k^2 \log \left(\frac{n_t}{k} \right) \log \left(\frac{n_r}{k} \right)$ without constant scaling in Fig. 5.1.

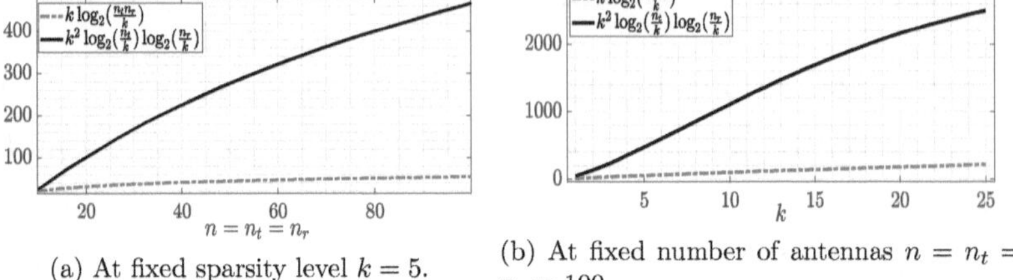

(a) At fixed sparsity level $k = 5$.

(b) At fixed number of antennas $n = n_t = n_r = 100$.

Figure 5.1: Unscaled asymptotic measurement lower bounds.

5.4.1 Main Results: A "Tight" Measurement Bound

In this section, we will derive the relationship between $k-$RIP constants of Kronecker product matrices and those of the blocks that form it. Then, using Theorem 5.3.2, we will derive an asymptotic lower bound on the number of rows of $\boldsymbol{G_v}$ and deduce its asymptotic behavior. We will finally show the tightness of our derived asymptotic bound using the solution framework in [67].

Optimum Measurement Length: Among all possible matrices which satisfy the RIP property, we are interested in the ones that have the least number of rows (since the number of rows equals the number of measurements). This leads to the notion of "*Optimum Measurement Length (OML)*". *We define OML as the smallest number of measurements such that the RIP property is satisfied.* OML is dependent on the length of unknown vectors n, the maximum sparsity level k and the $k-$RIP constant δ. Hence, we can define a function μ,

$$\mu : \mathcal{N} \times \mathcal{K} \times (0, 1) \rightarrow \mathbb{N}_0^+ \tag{5.4.3}$$

which maps the space of all possible values for n, k, and δ, given by[1] $\mathcal{N} \subseteq \mathbb{N}_0^+$, $\mathcal{K} \subseteq \mathbb{N}_0^+$ and $(0,1)$, respectively, to the corresponding OML quantity.

Now, let us focus on the special case of matrices which can be *arbitrarily* constructed. In such case, let μ be denoted by μ_a ('a' stands for Arbitrary matrix construction). We define μ_a to be the solution of the following optimization problem:

$$P2 : \underset{\boldsymbol{M_a} \in \mathbb{C}^{m_a \times n}}{\text{minimize}} \quad m_a \tag{5.4.4}$$
$$\text{subject to} \quad \boldsymbol{M_a} \in \mathcal{F}_\delta,$$

where $\mathcal{F}_\delta$ is the feasible set, and it is defined as

$$\mathcal{F}_\delta \triangleq \{ \boldsymbol{M_a} \in \mathbb{C}^{m_a \times n} : (1-\delta) \|\boldsymbol{x}\|_2^2 \leq \|\boldsymbol{M_a x}\|_2^2 \leq (1+\delta) \|\boldsymbol{x}\|_2^2,$$
$$\forall \boldsymbol{x} \in \mathbb{C}^n : \|\boldsymbol{x}\|_0 \leq k \}$$

Lemma 5.4.1. *Let n and k be fixed. Then, $\delta_1 \geq \delta_2$ implies $\mu_a(n,k,\delta_1) \leq \mu_a(n,k,\delta_2)$.*

Proof. The proof directly follows by observing that $\delta_1 \geq \delta_2$ implies that $\mathcal{F}_{\delta_2} \subseteq \mathcal{F}_{\delta_1}$. Since the problem is a minimization problem, then $\mu_a(n,k,\delta_1) \leq \mu_a(n,k,\delta_2)$. $\qquad\square$

Kronecker Product Matrices: The standard compressed sensing problem assumes that all elements of the sensing matrix are independently chosen. On the contrary, in sparse channel estimation, we are restricted to a specific sensing matrix structure, as shown in Eq. (5.3.11). The only free parameters in this sensing matrix are the tx-precoders $\boldsymbol{f_j}$ and the rx-combiners $\boldsymbol{w_i}$. This limitation suggests that more measurements may be needed to achieve the same RIP constant, compared to matrices whose elements are independently selected.

---

[1]We define $\mathbb{N}_0^+$ to be the set of non-negative integers.

At the heart of our results lies the relationship between the $k-$RIP constant of Kronecker product matrices and the $k-$RIP constants of the matrices that form them. We formally state this relationship in the following lemma.

Lemma 5.4.2 (RIP of Kronecker Products). *Let δ_a and δ_b be the $k-RIP$ constants of the matrices $\boldsymbol{A}$ and $\boldsymbol{B}$, respectively. Then, the $k-RIP$ constant of $\boldsymbol{A} \otimes \boldsymbol{B}$, denoted by δ, is bounded as*

$$\delta \geq \max\{\delta_a, \delta_b\} \tag{5.4.5}$$

A similar result to Lemma 5.4.2 was derived in [68], but under the stronger assumption of matrices with normalized columns. Our more general result implies that even if the normalized columns assumption is loosened, we still cannot obtain a matrix, through a Kronecker Product, which satisfies the RIP property with a constant smaller than the maximum of the $k-$RIP constants of the matrices that form it. The proof of Lemma 5.4.2 is provided in Appendix C.1.

A Generalized Bound: Recall Eq. (5.3.11). We will rewrite $\boldsymbol{G_v}$, for brevity, in terms of $\boldsymbol{M_t}$ and $\boldsymbol{M_r}$, where

$$\boldsymbol{M_t} \triangleq \left(\boldsymbol{F}^H \boldsymbol{U_t}\right)^* \in \mathbb{C}^{m_t \times n_t} \tag{5.4.6}$$

$$\boldsymbol{M_r} \triangleq \boldsymbol{W}^H \boldsymbol{U_r} \in \mathbb{C}^{m_r \times n_r} \tag{5.4.7}$$

Thus, we have $\boldsymbol{G_v} = \boldsymbol{M_t} \otimes \boldsymbol{M_r}$, and $m = m_t m_r$ is the number of rows of $\boldsymbol{G_v}$. Now, suppose that $\boldsymbol{G_v}$ satisfies $k-$RIP with constant $\delta \in (0,1)$. Then, both $\boldsymbol{M_t}$ and $\boldsymbol{M_r}$ must satisfy the $k-$RIP with constants $\delta_t \in (0,1)$ and $\delta_r \in (0,1)$, respectively. To show that this is true, assume, without loss of generality (w.l.o.g.), that there does not exist $\delta_t \in (0,1)$ such that $\boldsymbol{M_t}$ satisfies $k-$RIP. Then, there exists a vector $\boldsymbol{v}$ with $\|\boldsymbol{v}\|_0 \leq k$ such that $\boldsymbol{M_t}\boldsymbol{v} = \boldsymbol{0}$, which implies the existence of at least k dependent columns of

M_t, call them $a_{t1}, a_{t2}, \ldots, a_{tk}$. In turn, there exists at least k dependent columns in G_v (Let a_{r1} be a column in M_r, then the columns $a_{t1} \otimes a_{r1}, a_{t2} \otimes a_{r1}, \ldots, a_{tk} \otimes a_{r1}$ are dependent). Hence, $\nexists \delta \in (0,1)$ such that G_v satisfies $k-$RIP with a constant δ. Thus, we arrive at a contradiction. Further, by Lemma 5.4.2, we have that $\delta \geq \max\{\delta_t, \delta_r\}$.

Since M_t and M_r can be arbitrarily constructed, then we can lower bound m_t and m_r by their OML values as follows

$$m_t \geq \mu_a(n_t, k, \delta_t) \overset{(i)}{\geq} \mu_a(n_t, k, \delta) \tag{5.4.8}$$

$$m_t \geq \mu_a(n_r, k, \delta_r) \overset{(ii)}{\geq} \mu_a(n_r, k, \delta) \tag{5.4.9}$$

where inequalities (i) and (ii) follow from Lemma 5.4.1. Thus, it follows that the number of rows of G_v, m, is bounded as

$$m \geq \mu_a(n_t, k, \delta) \times \mu_a(n_r, k, \delta). \tag{5.4.10}$$

Recall that $\mu_a(\cdot)$ is the value that solves problem P1.

Remark 5.4.0.1. *The implication of Inequality (5.4.10) is that the number of measurements needed for estimating a sparse MIMO channel, Q, is at least equal to (but possibly higher) than the product of the number of measurements needed to solve the following two sub-problems:*

- *The first is a Single-Input Multiple-Output (SIMO), $1 \times n_r$ channel, with M_t^* as sensing matrix.*

- *The second is a Multiple-Input Single-Output (MISO), $n_t \times 1$ channel, with M_r as sensing matrix,* *where the sparsity level of both channels is $\leq k$. These two sub-problems are special cases of the original problem, whose measurement equations are shown in Eq. (2.0.13) and Eq. (2.0.14), respectively. The only difference is the conjugation of $\boldsymbol{M_t}$.*

The bound we derive in Eq. (5.4.10) highlights the dependence on the channel dimensions n_t and n_r, the maximum sparsity level k and a measure, δ, of how much information the measurements preserve about the channel. This bound, however, is not explicit, but we can use Theorem 5.3.2 to derive a more concrete lower bound for $\mu_a(\cdot)$. This leads to our main result:

Theorem 5.4.1 (Main Theorem). *Fix $\delta \in (0,1)$. If $\boldsymbol{G_v}$ in Eq. (5.3.11) satisfies RIP with order $2k$ and constant δ, then the number of measurements m is asymptotically bounded as:*

$$m = \Omega\left(k^2 \log\left(\frac{n_t}{k}\right) \log\left(\frac{n_r}{k}\right)\right) \tag{5.4.11}$$

Proof. Since $\mu_a(n_t, 2k, \delta)$ and $\mu_a(n_r, 2k, \delta)$ are obtained by solving the problem $P1$ (with their respective n_t, n_r and δ values), then there exists matrices $\boldsymbol{X_t}$ and $\boldsymbol{X_r}$, with dimensions $\mu_a(n_t, 2k, \delta) \times n_t$ and $\mu_a(n_r, 2k, \delta) \times n_r$ which satisfy $2k-$RIP with constant δ. Thus, it follows by Theorem 5.3.2 that:

$$\mu_a(n_t, 2k, \delta) \geq c_\delta 2k \log\left(\frac{n_t}{2k}\right) \tag{5.4.12}$$

$$\mu_a(n_r, 2k, \delta) \geq c_\delta 2k \log\left(\frac{n_r}{2k}\right) \tag{5.4.13}$$

Therefore, by Eq. (5.4.10), the following follows

$$m = m_t m_r \geq 4c_\delta^2 k^2 \log\left(\frac{n_t}{2k}\right) \log\left(\frac{n_r}{2k}\right) \tag{5.4.14}$$

Finally, let $c = 0.5$ and recall that the ratio $\dfrac{n_t}{k}$ increases (by assumption). Then, there exists $n_{t0} \in \mathbb{N}$ such that $\log(\dfrac{n_t}{2k}) \geq c\log(\dfrac{n_t}{k})$ for all $n_t \geq n_{t0}$. Similarly, there exists $n_{r0} \in \mathbb{N}$ such that $\log(\dfrac{n_r}{2k}) \geq c\log(\dfrac{n_r}{k})$ for all $n_r \geq n_{r0}$. Then, it follows that $m \geq 4c^2 c_\delta^2 k^2 \log\left(\dfrac{n_t}{k}\right) \log\left(\dfrac{n_r}{k}\right)$ where $4c^2 c_\delta^2 = c_\delta^2$ is a constant, from which Eq. (5.4.11) follows. $\qquad\qquad\square$

5.4.2 Tightness of the Measurement Bound

To argue that the measurement lower bound in Theorem 5.4.1 is tight, we will show that there exists a solution, based on [67], which yields sensing matrices that satisfy $2k-$RIP with constants $\in (0,1)$ and with $m \in \Theta\left(k^2 \log\left(\dfrac{n_t}{k}\right) \log\left(\dfrac{n_r}{k}\right)\right)$. We briefly discuss the measurement framework of [67] next.

In [67], a source-coding-based framework for the sparse MIMO channel estimation problem is developed. This solution proposes a method for obtaining a small number of measurements that are sufficient to estimate the channel. Such measurements are designed based on two carefully chosen binary linear source codes, C_t and C_r. These codes dictate the design of tx-precoders (using C_t) and rx-combiners (using C_r) and produce real-valued measurement (sensing) matrices, namely, $\boldsymbol{H_t}$ (of size $m_t \times n_t$) and $\boldsymbol{H_r}$ (of size $m_r \times n_r$), respectively. The matrix $\boldsymbol{H_t}$ can estimate $k-$sparse MISO channel vectors (i.e., produces unique measurements), while $\boldsymbol{H_r}$ can estimate $k-$sparse SIMO channels. Hence, the spark of both matrices is greater than $2k$ (by Theorem 5.3.1). Measurements are then obtained using all combinations of m_t tx-precoders and m_r rx-combiners, and can be arranged as $\boldsymbol{y_v} = \boldsymbol{H_v} \boldsymbol{q}_v^a + \boldsymbol{n_v}$ where $\boldsymbol{H_v} = \boldsymbol{H_t} \otimes \boldsymbol{H_r}$. By Lemma C.4.1 (in Appendix C.4), we have that $\mathrm{spark}(\boldsymbol{H_v}) > 2k$. Hence, either $\boldsymbol{H_v}$ or a scaled version of it satisfies $2k-$RIP with a constant $\delta_h \in (0,1)$. This measurement framework is shown to produce a number of measurements, m, that is lower bounded as:

$$m \geq \underline{m} \triangleq \underbrace{\left\lceil \log_2 \left(\sum_{i=0}^{k} \binom{n_r}{i} \right) \right\rceil}_{\leq m_t} \underbrace{\left\lceil \log_2 \left(\sum_{i=0}^{k} \binom{n_t}{i} \right) \right\rceil}_{\leq m_r}. \tag{5.4.15}$$

This lower bound is achievable with equality for specific examples as shown in [67]. However, it is not immediately clear how this bound compares to our bound in Eq. (5.4.11). The following lemma sheds more light on this issue:

Lemma 5.4.3. *The asymptotic behavior of $\underline{m}$, defined in Eq. (5.4.15) follows:* $\underline{m} = \Theta\left(k^2 \log\left(\frac{n_t}{k} \right) \log\left(\frac{n_r}{k} \right) \right)$.

This is the same asymptotic behavior as the lower bound in Theorem 5.4.1. The proof is provided in Appendix C.2. Next, we will examine a specific solution based on the family of BCH codes, which results in a number of measurements upper bounded as $m = O\left(k^2 \log\left(\frac{n_t}{k} \right) \log\left(\frac{n_r}{k} \right) \right)$.

Example 5.4.1 (BCH codes). *Although BCH codes are natively error-correcting codes, they can be used as syndrome-source-codes, as well[2]. By the properties of BCH codes, we have that for any positive integers $t \geq 3$ and $k < 2^{t-1}$, there exists a binary BCH code with: i) block length $n = 2^t - 1$, ii) minimum distance $d_{min} \geq 2k+1$ (hence, it can correct up to k errors), and iii) a number of parity check bits $m \leq tk = k\log_2(n+1)$. Using BCH codes to design C_t and C_r, we obtain a solution whose number of measurements is upper bounded according to the following lemma:*

---

[2] A linear block error-correcting code (LBC) can be utilized as a syndrome source code which can uniquely compress sequences that contain a number of 1's less than or equal to the number of correctable errors of the used code [69]. The parity check matrix of the LBC code is used as the generator matrix for the source code. Hence, the number of parity bits of the LBC code is the length of the compressed sequences for the corresponding source code.

Lemma 5.4.4. *The number of measurements achievable using BCH codes in the framework of [67] is asymptotically bounded as $m = O\left(k^2 \log\left(\frac{n_t}{k}\right) \log\left(\frac{n_r}{k}\right)\right)$.*

The proof depends on constructing syndrome source codes with arbitrary block lengths, and is provided in Appendix C.3.

Among all solutions in [67], we are interested in the ones whose number of measurements, m, is closest to $\underline{m}$. These solutions are *"Optimum"* in the sense of reducing the number of measurements. Recall that $\underline{m}$ is the lower bound of all solutions based on [67] (see Eq. (5.4.15)). The following theorem shows that these optimum solutions scale similarly to $\underline{m}$, which in turn shows that the lower bound of Theorem 5.4.1 is tight.

Theorem 5.4.2. *The number of measurements of "Optimum Solutions" of [67] scales as $m = \Theta\left(k^2 \log\left(\frac{n_t}{k}\right) \log\left(\frac{n_r}{k}\right)\right)$*

Proof. By Lemma 5.4.3, we have that all solutions, including the optimal, have $m = \Omega\left(k^2 \log\left(\frac{n_t}{k}\right) \log\left(\frac{n_r}{k}\right)\right)$. Moreover, Lemma 5.4.4 shows that solutions based on BCH codes result in $m = O\left(k^2 \log\left(\frac{n_t}{k}\right) \log\left(\frac{n_r}{k}\right)\right)$. Since optimal solutions have a number of measurements smaller than or equal to those obtained by BCH codes, then they also have the same asymptotic upper bound. Therefore, optimal solutions have $m = \Theta\left(k^2 \log\left(\frac{n_t}{k}\right) \log\left(\frac{n_r}{k}\right)\right)$ follows. $\qquad\square$

Remark 5.4.2.1. *Even though we have shown that the bound of Theorem 5.4.1 is tight, we have demonstrated this tightness in the asymptotic regime of n and k. The dependence on the RIP constant, δ, however, remains an open question.*

5.5 Conclusion

In this chapter, we study the fundamental lower bound governing the number of measurements, required for estimating sparse, large-MIMO channels. We consider a simple analog transceiver, where each channel measurements is obtained using a unique combination of beamforming vectors at the transmitter and receiver. We show that the currently known lower bound on number of measurements, i.e., $\Omega\left(k\log\left(\frac{n_r n_t}{k}\right)\right)$ is loose. We then derive a tight lower measurement bound, which scales asymptotically as $\Omega\left(k^2\log\left(\frac{n_t}{k}\right)\log\left(\frac{n_r}{k}\right)\right)$. The tightness of our derived bound is demonstrated by showing that there exists a solution with $m = O\left(k^2\log\left(\frac{n_t}{k}\right)\log\left(\frac{n_r}{k}\right)\right)$.

CHAPTER 6

CONCLUSION AND FUTURE WORK

In this work, we study the estimation problem of sparse channels that have large dimensions, which are prevalent in high-frequency communication systems. This problem is fundamentally different from classical channel estimation problems, due to the combination of the large antenna arrays used, and the deviation from the classical, expensive and power-hungry fully-digital transceiver architectures. Under these system settings, traditional solutions would necessitate a large number of measurements, which would in turn result in a prohibitively large estimation overhead that would render those systems impractical.

In this book, we use binary codes to help design channel measurements that make the estimation process more efficient. To elaborate, we propose solving the channel estimation problem as a path discovery problem. Since the channel is sparse, it only contains few significant paths. Identifying the angular directions of those paths along with their path gains is the core of the problem, which we solve by designing the channel measurements to behave in a way similar to syndrome decoding in binary channel coding. The primary idea here is that path discovery in the angular domain, and error discovery in a codeword (in channel coding) are fundamentally similar. That is, in syndrome decoding, we are able to construct a unique syndrome of small size for every error sequence. Similarly, we show that by appropriate code selection, we can obtain measurements which act as unique channel syndromes for every possible channel. Then, mapping the obtained measurements (i.e. the channel syndrome) back to the channels gives us our channel estimate. The code selection is straight-forward: If we have n antennas and k paths, then we need a code which can correct k errors in a codeword of length n.

We then set out to find the lower bound on the number of measurements necessary for channel estimation under our framework. The channel coding analogy, however, is not well-suited to obtaining this bound. Hence, we construct another analogy to beam discovery using source coding, which facilitates solving the lower bound problem. Precisely, we show that channel measurements can be designed to mimic a compressed version of the channel, where compression is done using generator matrices of binary linear source codes. Therefore, the lower bound on the number of measurements is the lower bound on compression, which can be derived using the Shannon Bound. The measurement bound we obtain is $m \geq \underline{m} \triangleq \left\lceil \log_2 \left(\sum_{i=0}^{k} \binom{n_r}{i} \right) \right\rceil \left\lceil \log_2 \left(\sum_{i=0}^{k} \binom{n_t}{i} \right) \right\rceil$, where n_r and n_t are the numbers of RX and TX antennas, k is the number of paths and m is the number of paths.

Since our bound, $\underline{m}$, is based on the binary coding framework, this opens the door to another question as to whether other solutions (i.e., not based on binary coding) may require fewer measurements. To answer this question, we need to understand the relationship between our solution's lower bound and that of any general solution. Thus, we derive another general measurement lower bound, which is shown to be $m = \Omega \left(k^2 \log \left(\frac{n_t}{k} \right) \log \left(\frac{n_r}{k} \right) \right)$. This is significantly tighter than the previously known bound of $m = \Omega \left(k \log \left(\frac{n}{k} \right) \right)$. We also show that $\underline{m} = \Theta \left(k^2 \log \left(\frac{n_t}{k} \right) \log \left(\frac{n_r}{k} \right) \right)$. Hence, in the asymptotic regime, both our binary-coding-based bound and the general bound scale exactly the same. We also show that our bounds are tight by showing that there exists a solution which achieves those bounds.

6.1 Key outcomes

- Despite the fact that most existing solutions for the channel estimation problem rely on some form of randomized measurements to reduce the estimation overhead, we show that we can still achieve a significant measurement reduction using a deterministic approach.

- Not only do we adopt a deterministic measurement approach, but our measurements constitute a binary decision as to whether include or exclude signals coming from a particular angular direction. This makes the design of beamforming vectors significantly easier and resilient to errors and imperfections in electronic components.

- Although our binary-coding-based solution limits the space of measurement matrices to those that resemble binary codes, the measurement process remains as efficient as any general solution, in the sense of reducing the number of measurements. This is evident by the identical lower measurement bounds of our proposed solution, and the general solution.

- In addition, when compared to classical compressed sensing methods, our solution demonstrates superior performance at all levels of SNR, especially for low resolution ADCs. Performance of compressed sensing is very sensitive to quantization noise and only improves as the ADC resolution increases.

6.2 Future Work

Coding for Beam Tracking: In this dissertation, we have focused on the Initial Link Establishment problem, which is essentially a channel estimation problem with limited prior knowledge about the channel. Once the link has been established, we need to maintain the viability of the active link. This is known as beam/channel tracking. The aim of this problem is to keep track of incremental changes in the channel. It can be thought of as channel estimation with detailed prior knowledge about the channel. This problem can be formulated in a way similar to source coding. However, unlike our previous proposition of only using linear codes, we can expand the space of codes used to variable-length codes. Variable length codes allows for embedding the information known about the channel into the channel estimation problem. The way it would work is that the most likely channels could be estimated using fewer measurements compared less likely ones. This also is a type of adaptive channel estimation in which future measurements are based on information obtained from previous measurements.

Location Privacy: The large-MIMO systems, necessary for combating the sever losses at high frequency, create another challenge all of their own. That is, channel estimation of such systems reveal a very detailed picture of the communication environment. This information, while necessary for efficient communication, raises the risk that any two communicating nodes can, with incredible accuracy, locate the physical location of each other. Exposing users' location can have tremendous impact on their security since it not only exposes their locations but it can also reveal their habits, routines, beliefs, political affiliations, etc. Hence, protecting this information is of fundamental importance. A trade-off between the location privacy (as a function of channel state information) and the quality of communication links exists. We will study this trade-off in the future by posing it as a constrained optimization problem with the constraint being the level of desired location privacy.

APPENDIX A: PROOFS FOR CHAPTER 3

A.1 Proof of Proposition 3.5.1

Proof. We need to show that

$$\left\| y^{\nu}_{s_1} - y^{\nu}_{s_2} \right\| \geq \left\| y_{s_1} - y_{s_2} \right\| \tag{A.1.1}$$

$$\iff \left\| H^{\nu} \left(q^a_1 - q^a_2 \right) \right\|^2 \geq \left\| H \left(q^a_1 - q^a_2 \right) \right\|^2 \tag{A.1.2}$$

Let $v = q^a_1 - q^a_2$, then, Eq. (A.1.2) is true if and only if

$$\left(H^{\nu} v \right)^T \left(H^{\nu} v \right) \geq \left(H^{\nu} v \right)^T \left(H v \right) \tag{A.1.3}$$

$$\iff v^T \left(\left(H^{\nu} \right)^T H^{\nu} - H^T H \right) v \geq 0 \tag{A.1.4}$$

$$\iff \left(H^{\nu} \right)^T H^{\nu} - H^T H \succeq 0, \tag{A.1.5}$$

i.e., $(\boldsymbol{H}^{\nu})^T \boldsymbol{H}^{\nu} - \boldsymbol{H}^T \boldsymbol{H}$ is positive semi-definite. Suppose $\boldsymbol{G_c}$ is of size $m \times m_c$. Since $\boldsymbol{G_c}$ is in standard form[1] (by assumption), then it can be written as a block matrix:

$$\boldsymbol{G_c} = \left(\boldsymbol{I} \ \middle| \ \boldsymbol{P} \right), \tag{A.1.6}$$

where $\boldsymbol{I}$ is the $m \times m$ identity matrix and $\boldsymbol{P}$ is of size $m \times m_c - m$. Then, we can find $\boldsymbol{H}^{\nu}$ to be given as

$$\boldsymbol{H}^{\nu} = \boldsymbol{G}_c^T \boldsymbol{H} \quad (\text{mod } 2) \ = \begin{pmatrix} \boldsymbol{I} \\ \boldsymbol{P}^T \end{pmatrix} \boldsymbol{H} \quad (\text{mod } 2) \tag{A.1.7}$$

$$= \begin{pmatrix} \boldsymbol{H} \\ \boldsymbol{P}^T \boldsymbol{H} \end{pmatrix} \quad (\text{mod } 2) = \begin{pmatrix} \boldsymbol{H} \\ \boldsymbol{P}_m \end{pmatrix} \tag{A.1.8}$$

where $\boldsymbol{P}_m = \boldsymbol{P}^T \boldsymbol{H} \ (\text{mod } 2)$. Hence, we have that

$$(\boldsymbol{H}^{\nu})^T \boldsymbol{H}^{\nu} = \boldsymbol{H}^T \boldsymbol{H} + \boldsymbol{P}_m^T \boldsymbol{P}_m \tag{A.1.9}$$

Hence, we get that $\forall \boldsymbol{v} \in \mathbb{C}^n$,

$$\boldsymbol{v}^T \left((\boldsymbol{H}^{\nu})^T \boldsymbol{H}^{\nu} - \boldsymbol{H}^T \boldsymbol{H} \right) \boldsymbol{v} = \boldsymbol{v}^T \boldsymbol{P}_m^T \boldsymbol{P}_m \boldsymbol{v} \tag{A.1.10}$$

$$= \|\boldsymbol{P}_m \boldsymbol{v}\|^2 \geq 0 \tag{A.1.11}$$

Hence, Eq. (A.1.5) is satisfied, which completes the proof. $\qquad \square$

---

[1] For any LBC code $C1$, we can find an equivalent *systematic* code $C2$ using row reduction and column reordering operations [53]. A systematic code is an LBC with generator matrix structure given by Eq. (A.1.6).

APPENDIX B: PROOFS FOR CHAPTER 4

B.1 Proof Of Lemma 4.4.1

Proof. Consider a set of n−dimensional linearly independent vectors, $v_1, \ldots, v_m$ defined over $\mathbb{F}_2$. Then, construct a matrix $M_{\mathbb{F}_2}$ whose columns are $v_1, \ldots, v_m$. Since v_i's are independent, then $M_{\mathbb{F}_2}$ has full column rank, i.e., $M_{\mathbb{F}_2}$ is left-invertible over $\mathbb{F}_2$ ($m \leq n$). Thus $M_{\mathbb{F}_2}$ has an $m \times m$ minor, call it $A_{\mathbb{F}_2}$ whose determinant is non-zero. Now consider the matrix M, defined over $\mathbb{C}$, whose elements are the 0 and 1 real scalars corresponding to $0_{\mathbb{F}_2}$ and $1_{\mathbb{F}_2}$ values of $M_{\mathbb{F}_2}$. Let A be its minor corresponding to $A_{\mathbb{F}_2}$ of $M_{\mathbb{F}_2}$. By lemma B.2.1 (in Appendix B.2), we have $\det(A) \neq 0$. Thus, M is also left-invertible, hence its columns are linearly independent. $\qquad\square$

B.2 Lemma B.2.1

Lemma B.2.1. *Let $A_{\mathbb{F}}$ and A be $n \times n$ matrices defined over $\mathbb{F}_2$ and $\mathbb{R}$, respectively. Let $a_{\mathbb{F}i,j}$, the elements of $A_{\mathbb{F}}$, be scalars in $\{0_{\mathbb{F}_2}, 1_{\mathbb{F}_2}\}$, while $a_{i,j}$ the elements of A, be scalars in $\{0,1\} \subseteq \mathbb{R}$. Suppose that $A_{\mathbb{F}}$ has non-zero determinant, i.e., $\det(A_{\mathbb{F}}) \neq 0_{\mathbb{F}_2}$. If we define A such that $a_{i,j} = 0$ if $a_{\mathbb{F}i,j} = 0_{\mathbb{F}_2}$, and $a_{i,j} = 1$ if $a_{\mathbb{F}i,j} = 1_{\mathbb{F}_2}$ for all $1 \leq i, j \leq n$. Then, $\det(A) \neq 0$.*

Proof. Recall that the determinant of a square matrix defined over a commutative ring is given by the Leibniz formula [70]. Since $\mathbb{F}_2$ is a finite field (with 2 elements), it constitutes a commutative ring. Moreover, $\mathbb{R}$ is a commutative ring [70]. Therefore, both determinants of $\boldsymbol{A}_{\mathbb{F}}$ and $\boldsymbol{A}$ can be computed using the same exact formula. Since, finite field arithmetic over the prime field $\mathbb{Z}_2$ is the integers *modulo* 2, then we can write $\det(\boldsymbol{A}_{\mathbb{F}}) = \det(\boldsymbol{A}) \mod 2$. Thus, $\exists q \in \mathbb{Z}$ (the set of integers), such that $\det(\boldsymbol{A}) = q \times 2 + \det(\boldsymbol{A}_{\mathbb{F}}) = q \times 2 + 1$, were the latter equation follows from the fact that $\det(\boldsymbol{A}_{\mathbb{F}}) \neq 0_{\mathbb{F}_2} \iff \det(\boldsymbol{A}_{\mathbb{F}})=1_{\mathbb{F}_2}$. Therefore, $\det(\boldsymbol{A})$ *is an odd integer*, which implies that $\det(\boldsymbol{A}) \neq 0$, concluding our proof. $\qquad\square$

B.3 Proof of Proposition 4.4.2

Proof. We will prove that adding an extra column $\boldsymbol{p} \in \mathbb{R}^m$ to any **full rank** matrix $\boldsymbol{M}$ of size $m \times k$ with $m \leq k$ (i.e., $\operatorname{rank}(\boldsymbol{M})=m$) *does not reduce* its singular values.

Let $\boldsymbol{M_p} = \left(\boldsymbol{M} \mid \boldsymbol{p}\right)$ be an $m \times k{+}1$ matrix. Then, we can obtain the singular values of $\boldsymbol{M_p}$ as the positive square roots of the eigenvalues of $\boldsymbol{M_p}\boldsymbol{M_p^T}$, which can be written as:

$$\boldsymbol{M_p}\boldsymbol{M_p^T} = \left(\boldsymbol{M} \mid \boldsymbol{p}\right)\left(\boldsymbol{M} \mid \boldsymbol{p}\right)^T = \boldsymbol{M}\boldsymbol{M}^T + \boldsymbol{p}\boldsymbol{p}^T \tag{B.3.1}$$

Since $\boldsymbol{p}\boldsymbol{p}^T \succeq 0$ (i.e., positive semidefinite), then we must have $\boldsymbol{M_p}\boldsymbol{M_p^T} - \boldsymbol{M}\boldsymbol{M}^T \succeq 0$. Let $\sigma_i(\cdot)$ denote the ith largest singular value of a matrix. Then, we have $\sigma_i\left(\boldsymbol{M_p}\boldsymbol{M_p^T}\right) \geq \sigma_i\left(\boldsymbol{M}\boldsymbol{M}^T\right) \ \forall i = 1,\ldots,m$, which implies

$$\implies \sigma_{\min}\left(\boldsymbol{M_p}\boldsymbol{M_p^T}\right) \geq \sigma_{\min}\left(\boldsymbol{M}\boldsymbol{M}^T\right) \implies \sigma_{\min}\left(\boldsymbol{M_p}\right) \geq \sigma_{\min}\left(\boldsymbol{M}\right) \tag{B.3.2}$$

Define $\boldsymbol{G}^{(i)} \triangleq \left(\boldsymbol{g}_1 \ \ \boldsymbol{g}_2 \ \ \cdots \ \ \boldsymbol{g}_i\right)$, where $\boldsymbol{g}_j$ is the jth column of $\boldsymbol{G}$. Then, by sequentially applying the result shown in Eq. (B.3.2) (by adding columns of $\boldsymbol{P}$ in Eq. (4.4.16)), we obtain

$$
\begin{aligned}
\sigma_{\min}\left(\boldsymbol{G}\right) &= \sigma_{\min}\left(\boldsymbol{G}^{(n)}\right) \geq \sigma_{\min}\left(\boldsymbol{G}^{(n-1)}\right) \geq \cdots \\
&\geq \sigma_{\min}\left(\boldsymbol{G}^{(m+1)}\right) \geq \sigma_{\min}\left(\boldsymbol{G}^{(m)}\right) = \sigma_{\min}\left(\boldsymbol{I}_m\right) = 1 \quad \square
\end{aligned}
\tag{B.3.3}
$$

APPENDIX C: PROOFS FOR CHAPTER 5

C.1 Proof of Lemma 5.4.2

Proof. Let $A \in \mathbb{R}^{m_a \times n_a}$ and $B \in \mathbb{R}^{m_b \times n_b}$. Denote by a_i the ith column of A and let $a_{i,j}$ be its jth element. And define $C \triangleq A \otimes B$. Denote by δ_c the $k-$RIP constant of C.

We will first show that $\delta_c \geq \delta_b$. To that end, let us define the sets $\mathcal{X}_c$ and $\mathcal{X}_b$ as:

$$\mathcal{X}_c \triangleq \{x_c \in \mathbb{R}^{n_a n_b} : \|x_c\|_0 \leq k\} \tag{C.1.1}$$

$$\mathcal{X}_b \triangleq \{x_b \in \mathbb{R}^{n_b} : \|x_b\|_0 \leq k\} \tag{C.1.2}$$

Since δ_c is the $k-$RIP constant of C, then $\forall x_c \in \mathcal{X}_c$ we have

$$(1 - \delta_c) \|x_c\|^2 \leq \|C x_c\|^2 \leq (1 + \delta_c) \|x_c\|^2 \tag{C.1.3}$$

Now, we will focus our attention on a smaller class of vectors $x_c^{(b)}$, which constitute a strict subset of $\mathcal{X}_c$, defined as follows

$$x_c^{(b)} \triangleq \left(b^T \quad 0^T \quad \ldots \quad 0^T \right)^T, \tag{C.1.4}$$

where $b \in \mathcal{X}_b$ and $x_c^{(b)} \in \mathbb{R}^{n_a n_b}$. Then, by construction, $x_c^{(b)} \in \mathcal{X}_c$, and $\left\|x_c^{(b)}\right\| = \|b\|$.

Now, observe that $\left\|C x_c^{(b)}\right\|^2$ is

$$\left\|C x_c^{(b)}\right\|^2 = \left\|(A \otimes B) x_c^{(b)}\right\|^2 = \sum_{i=1}^{n_a} |a_{i,1}|^2 \|Bb\|^2 \tag{C.1.5}$$

$$= \|a_1\|^2 \|Bb\|^2 \tag{C.1.6}$$

Since δ_b is the $k-$RIP constant of B, then $\forall b \in \mathcal{X}_b$ we have

$$\|a_1\|^2 (1 - \delta_b) \|b\|^2 \leq \underbrace{\|a_1\|^2 \|Bb\|^2}_{=\left\|C x_c^{(b)}\right\|^2} \leq \|a_1\|^2 (1 + \delta_b) \|b\|^2 \tag{C.1.7}$$

Since (i) the space of all possible constructions of $x_c^{(b)}$ is a strict subset of $\mathcal{X}_c$, and since (ii) δ_b is the smallest constant such that Eq. (C.1.7) holds, then the following two equations must always hold true

$$(1 - \delta_c) \|b\|^2 \leq \|a_1\|^2 (1 - \delta_b) \|b\|^2 \tag{B1}$$

$$\|a_1\|^2 (1 + \delta_b) \|b\|^2 \leq (1 + \delta_c) \|b\|^2 \tag{B2}$$

If $\|a_1\|^2 \leq 1$, then from Eq. (B1) we have $\delta_c \geq \delta_b$. Otherwise, if $\|a_1\|^2 \geq 1$, then from Eq. (B2) we have $\delta_c \geq \delta_b$. Therefore, $\delta_b \leq \delta_c$ is always true. Now, define $C' \triangleq B \otimes A$. By the properties of the Kronecker product, we know that there exist two "Permutation" matrices, call them P_ρ and P_c, such that:

$$C' = P_\rho C P_c = P_\rho (A \otimes B) P_c, \tag{C.1.8}$$

where P_ρ permutes the rows of C, and P_c permutes the columns of $P_\rho C$. Then, we have that

$$\|\boldsymbol{C}'\boldsymbol{x_c}\| = \|\boldsymbol{P}_\rho \boldsymbol{C}\boldsymbol{P_c}\boldsymbol{x_c}\| \overset{(i)}{=} \|\boldsymbol{C}\boldsymbol{P_c}\boldsymbol{x_c}\| \,. \tag{C.1.9}$$

Also, observe that if $\boldsymbol{x_c} \in \mathcal{X}_c$, then $\boldsymbol{P_c}\boldsymbol{x_c}$ has the same sparsity level as $\boldsymbol{x_c}$ and hence it lies in $\mathcal{X}_c$, as well. Therefore, it follows that

$$(1 - \delta_c)\,\|\boldsymbol{x_c}\|^2 \leq \underbrace{\|\boldsymbol{C}'\boldsymbol{x_c}\|^2}_{=\|\boldsymbol{C}\boldsymbol{P_c}\boldsymbol{x_c}\|^2} \leq (1 + \delta_c)\,\|\boldsymbol{x_c}\|^2 \,, \tag{C.1.10}$$

which shows that both $\boldsymbol{C}$ and $\boldsymbol{C}'$ have the same $k-$RIP constant δ_c. Then, it follows that $\delta_c \geq \delta_a$. Therefore, $\delta_c \geq \max\{\delta_a, \delta_b\}$, which concludes our proof. $\qquad\square$

C.2 Proof Of Lemma 5.4.3

Proof. First, observe that $\binom{n}{i} < \binom{n}{k}$ for all $0 \leq i < k$ such that $k < \dfrac{n+1}{2}$. Thus, for $k < \dfrac{n+1}{2}$, we have that

$$\sum_{i=0}^{k} \binom{n}{i} \leq (k+1) \binom{n}{k} \tag{C.2.1}$$

By taking the logarithm of the previous equation, we get

$$\Rightarrow \log\left(\sum_{i=0}^{k} \binom{n}{i}\right) \leq \log\left(k+1\right) + \log\binom{n}{k} \tag{C.2.2}$$

$$\leq \log\left(k+1\right) + k\log\left(\frac{n}{k}\right) + k\log e, \tag{C.2.3}$$

where (C.2.3) follows from the following popular bounds on $\binom{n}{k}$ [71]

$$\left(\frac{n}{k}\right)^k \leq \binom{n}{k} \leq \left(\frac{ne}{k}\right)^k . \tag{C.2.4}$$

From (C.2.4) we also have that $\left(\frac{n}{k}\right)^k \leq \binom{n}{k} \leq \sum_{i=0}^{k}\binom{n}{i}$. This gives us the following upper and lower bounds on Υ where

$$\Upsilon \triangleq \left\lceil \log_2\left(\sum_{i=0}^{k}\binom{n}{i}\right)\right\rceil \tag{C.2.5}$$

$$k\log\left(\frac{n}{k}\right) \leq \Upsilon \leq \log(k+1) + k\log\left(\frac{n}{k}\right) + k\log e + 1 \tag{C.2.6}$$

Therefore, we have that Υ is in both $\Omega\left(k\log\frac{n}{k}\right)$ and $O\left(k\log\frac{n}{k}\right)$. Hence, $\Upsilon \in \Theta\left(k\log\frac{n}{k}\right)$. Finally, we can conclude that $\underline{\mathrm{m}} = \Upsilon|_{n=n_t}\Upsilon|_{n=n_r}$ is asymptotically bounded as

$$\underline{\mathrm{m}} = \Theta\left(k^2 \log\left(\frac{n_t}{k}\right)\log\left(\frac{n_r}{k}\right)\right) \qquad \square$$

C.3 Proof Of Lemma 5.4.4

Proof. First, we will show that $m_t \leq ck\log\frac{n_t}{k}$ for some $c > 0$. Let n_t be an arbitrary integer such that $n_t >= 7$. Then, there exists a positive integer $t \geq 3$ such that $2^t - 1 \leq n_t < 2^{t+1} - 1$. If $n_t = 2^t - 1$, then there exists a BCH code with a number of parity check bits m_t such that $m_t \leq k\log(n_t + 1)$. Hence, there exists a positive constant $c_0 \in \mathbb{R}$ such that $m_t \leq c_0 k\log(n_t)$. On the other hand, if $2^t - 1 < n_t < 2^{t+1} - 1$, then we can construct a linear block code of length n_t by shortening a BCH code with block length $n_t' = 2^{t+1}-1$ and number of parity check bits $m_t \leq k\log(n_t'+1)$. This shortening process leaves the number of parity bits intact, hence, we have that $m_t \leq k\log(n_t' + 1)$, but it removes $n_t' - n_t$ information bits from the codewords. Thus, we have

$$m_t \leq k\log\left(2^{t+1}\right) \leq \frac{4}{3}k\log\left(2^t\right) < \frac{4}{3}k\log\left(n_t + 1\right). \tag{C.3.1}$$

Now, recall that $n_t \geq k^{1+\epsilon}$, where $\epsilon > 0$ (by assumption). Then, we have that $\frac{1}{\epsilon} \log \frac{n_t}{k} \geq \log k$. Therefore,

$$\log(n_t) = \log\left(\frac{n_t}{k} \times k\right) = \left(\log\left(\frac{n_t}{k}\right) + \log(k)\right) \tag{C.3.2}$$

$$\leq \left(\log\left(\frac{n_t}{k}\right) + \frac{1}{\epsilon} \log \frac{n_t}{k}\right) = \left(1 + \frac{1}{\epsilon}\right) \log\left(\frac{n_t}{k}\right) \tag{C.3.3}$$

Thus, if follows that $m_t = O(k \log\left(\frac{n_t}{k}\right))$ for arbitrary $n_t \in \mathbb{N}$. Similarly, we have $m_r = O\left(k \log\left(\frac{n_r}{k}\right)\right)$. Thus, it follows that $m = O(k^2 \log\left(\frac{n_t}{k}\right) \log\left(\frac{n_r}{k}\right))$. $\qquad \square$

C.4   Spark of the Kronecker Product

Lemma C.4.1. *Let* $A \in \mathbb{C}^{m_a \times n_a}$ *and* $B \in \mathbb{C}^{m_b \times n_b}$ *be such that* $\min\{\mathrm{spark}(A), \mathrm{spark}(B)\} > k$. *Then,* $\mathrm{spark}(A \otimes B) > k$.

Proof. Let $(a_i)_{i=1}^{n_a}$ and $(b_j)_{j=1}^{n_b}$ be the columns of A and B, respectively. Since $\mathrm{spark}(A) > k$, then any k columns of A are linearly independent. Similarly, any k columns of B are also independent. Observe that any column of $A \otimes B$ is of the form $a_i \otimes b_j$. Pick any k columns of $A \otimes B$, i.e., $a_{p_1} \otimes b_{t_1}, a_{p_2} \otimes b_{t_2}, \ldots, a_{p_k} \otimes b_{t_k}$. We will show that $\sum_{i=1}^{k} \alpha_i a_{p_i} \otimes b_{t_i} = 0$ if and only if $\alpha_i = 0 \; \forall i$.

Assume w.l.o.g. that $a_{p_1} = \ldots = a_{p_{d_1}}, a_{p_{d_1+1}} = \ldots = a_{p_{d_2}}, \ldots, a_{p_{d_{l-1}+1}} = \ldots = a_{p_{d_l}}$. And define $r_{d_1} \triangleq \sum_{i=1}^{d_1} \alpha_i b_{t_i}, r_{d_2} \triangleq \sum_{i=d_1+1}^{d_2} \alpha_i b_{t_i}, \ldots, r_{d_l} \triangleq \sum_{i=d_{l-1}+1}^{d_l=k} \alpha_i b_{t_i}$. Then, we can rewrite $\sum_{i=1}^{k} \alpha_i a_{p_i} \otimes b_{t_i}$ as: $a_{pd_1} \otimes r_{d_1} + a_{pd_2} \otimes r_{d_2} + \cdots + a_{pd_l} \otimes r_{d_l}$. Suppose there exists at least one value i_0 such that $\alpha_{i_0} \neq 0$, then $\exists r_{d_i} \neq 0$ since all b_{t_i} are independent. Finally, since all a_{pd_i} are independent, then $\sum_{i=1}^{k} \alpha_i a_{p_i} \otimes b_{t_i} \neq 0$. Therefore, the k columns $(a_{p_i} \otimes b_{t_i})_{i=1}^{k}$, of $A \otimes B$, are independent. Hence, $\mathrm{spark}(A \otimes B) > k$. $\qquad \square$